FROM

Courtroom to Cucina

70 Authentic Recipes that Took Me From Litigation to Salivation

Danielle Caminiti

Photography by Danielle Caminiti and Kevin Dong
Designed by Danielle Caminiti and Joe Cutroni

ISBN: 9798770856484

Author: Danielle Caminiti
Designer: Joe Cutroni
Photographer: Danielle Caminiti & Kevin Dong
Food and Prop Stylist: Danielle Caminiti

www.haveucoveredinthekitchen.com

Dedication

This book is dedicated to my maternal and paternal grandparents, to my parents, who lovingly fed me physically, mentally, spiritually, and emotionally, and to my son Luca.

May you always treasure these recipes and I hope that someday you enjoy them with your own family.

My Great Grandmother, Antoinette Paladino, and neighbors at 78-80 Mulberry Street in Manhattan's Little Italy, celebrate the end of World War II in 1945. She lived above the store pictured, which was owned and operated by Carmine Adimando, my Grandfather's Uncle. Both my parents' families settled in Little Italy from Italy.

Table of Contents

Breakfast & Brunch

Appetizers

Table of Contents

Soups

Main Courses

Table of Contents

Sides

Desserts

Drinks

Foreword

When Danielle asked me to write a foreword for her new book, I felt privileged and delighted. I witnessed her enthusiasm for food becoming so much more than just a passion; it became a tasty book with 70 mouth-watering recipes, including my favorite "Linguine Alle Vongole."

Some of those recipes were passed on from her Great Grandfather to her "Nana" to her Mom, and I am sure each generation adds some savory notes, as we, the Italians, love to personalize our way of cooking and serving food.

Those recipes hold the history and tradition of an Italian family that moved to America with genuine dreams almost a century ago, and this is why I deeply understand this book's incredible value.

During one of the most challenging circumstances of our present time, Danielle Caminiti turned her table around, and took her love for food to the next level. She seduced her new fans (including me) for over a year with lovely pictures of her delectable and colorful recipes.

With elegance and grace, she invites us to eat with our eyes while her tasting team, formed by her son, family and friends, were the official inspectors of her heavenly recipes, a mix of comfort and fusion food.

Danielle's table is now full of tasty recipes and tantalizing dishes. Proving that you can always turn your table around, and unexpectedly, even the most challenging time can bring a new exciting chapter to your life. I want to invite you to "Brindiamo!" to Danielle Caminiti and her new cookbook, "From Courtroom to Cucina," a statement of optimism and belief that dreams can come true thanks to determination and passion.

Ornella Fado
Ornella Fado is the founder of OK PRODUCTIONS LLC, a production company based in New York City that produces high-quality TV shows such as Brindiamo!, Brindiamo! in My Kitchen, Brindiamo! on the Sea, and Brindiamo! International cuisine since 2005.

She is also the executive producer, writer, and hostess of such titles and the founder of the "Brindiamo! Channel" a linear channel on Samsung TV PLUS Italy, Huawei, Rakuten, LG, and rlaxx TV Italy. Brindiamo! is a groundbreaking television show about Italian food, Italian lifestyle, and fine Italian restaurants filmed in America, Italy, Bermuda, and Canada. She shares her passion and love for "Il Bel Paese" through her TV show Brindiamo! Selected series of Brindiamo! are streaming on various platforms worldwide, such as XUMO and Amazon Prime.

Ornella Fado
OK PRODUCTIONS LLC
Brindiamo! Channel TV PLUS ITALY, Samsung TV PLUS, Huawei, Rakuten, LG, and rlaxx TV Italy
Brindiamo! TV -NYC LIFE, XUMO, and Amazon Prime
www.ornellafado.com
www.brindiamoguide.com

Introduction

As far back as I can remember, I was always a foodie. Some may say that it's a birthright as an Italian-American, but I know plenty of people who have one foot in Italy and are far less passionate about all types of cuisines as I am. Similarly, I've met many non-Italian folks who are equally as food-obsessed as I am. Is it nature or nurture? Are foodies born or made? After much deliberation, I think that it's a little bit of both. I'm sure I was eating my fair share of chicken parm in utero (well, on second thought, maybe not, as my mother was always on some sort of diet). It's fair to say that I was definitely eating a good amount of chicken scarpariello in the womb. But it goes further than that.

I can tell you that my first memories of food coincide with my first memories of songs, around age 4 or 5. As my hippocampus was developing as a wee one, so was my sophisticated palate. Scientifically, the hippocampus, the area of the brain responsible for learning and memory, is not fully developed until about 2 1/2 years of age. However, due to childhood amnesia most people do not have declarative memories until they are around 3-5, sometimes a tad earlier sometimes later. The first songs I remember are "Another One Bites the Dust" by Queen, "Off the Wall" by Michael Jackson and "It's Still Rock and Roll to Me" by Billy Joel. Interestingly enough, my memories of these songs each come with a distinct memory of food.

"Off the Wall" was released in August 1979 when I was a month shy of 4. It reminds me of a Friday night in the basement of my house where we had a 38-record player. My sister and I always had friends over and would have dance contests down there. We used to ravage through my mom's storage closet and put on her old fringed vests of the 1960's as costumes for our colorful routines. I remember the smell of my mom cooking eggplant upstairs while we had the song on downstairs. My memory is fuzzy as to whether we actually had this on a record or whether it was playing on the stereo (it would have been my sister DJ'ing).

"It's Still Rock and Roll to Me" was released in May 1980. I was 4 3/4 years old. This song definitely reminds me of a Sunday dinner with my whole family with the aroma of sauce, meatballs, sausage and braciole ("gravy meat" as some would arguably say) permeating my surroundings. Like many Italian-American families, these gatherings occurred in my parents' basement. This was gold star standard for entertainment for Sunday Dinners and holidays. Ours had a full canary yellow kitchen and finished bathroom, and washer and dryer. My parents hosted virtually all our Sunday Dinners and holidays in their basement, unless we were having it with my Grandma Susie and Grandpa Vinny, my paternal grandparents, who lived in Little Italy in Manhattan. We lived in a Mother-Daughter house with my Nana and Grandfather, my maternal grandparents. In fact, we spent so much time in the basement that my grandparents had a telephone landline extension installed there so they could hear their upstairs phone ring while we were there. I often wondered why we even had ground floor, since we had 2 full rooms - with furniture covered in plastic - that we didn't even use. Ironically enough, "a living room" was one we couldn't really step foot in. My mother called the furniture in it "heirloom furniture." As a kid, I never knew what that meant when she said it in a raised tone, but to me it meant, go play downstairs.

"Another One Bites the Dust" was released in August 1980 and is reminiscent of my fifth birthday party in September of that year at a popular ice cream shop called Farrell's in the Staten Island Mall near where I grew up on Staten Island with my parents and older sister. I remember being filled with excitement about this party, not only because all my friends in and out of school were going to be there, but because, as the birthday girl, I knew I had carte blanche to pick out whatever candy sticks and ice cream I wanted from the candy store in front of the eatery. We pulled up to the place in my dad's pea-green Ford Torino and playing on the radio was none other than "Another One Bites the Dust." I distinctly remember rolling down the window to be greeted by a rowdy group of the boys on my block, who were invited to the party, standing outside goofing around as my dad turned the dial to make the radio louder. But my mind wasn't really on them so much as the root beer and green apple sticks I wanted dibs on as soon as we got in the place.

I digress...the common denominator in all these memories of music and family was food. Food brings people to the table and food brings people together. We grew up with humble beginnings. We weren't rich and we weren't poor, but we always had enough. My parents spared no expense in ensuring that we ate well and tried new things. There was no such thing as a "Children's Menu" when my sister and I ordered food. I'll admit it, the road wasn't always smooth.

There were times I was threatened by one or both parents tag teamed to try foods I was reluctant to try as a kid. Chicken fingers and French fries were not even part of our family-vocabulary. Instead, my parents resorted to Jedi mind tricks, reverse psychology and strong-arm tactics for us to, for example, taste that calamari ring, try that mussel or sample that scungilli.

My mother sternly saying, "try that and if you like it you're not getting anymore" was my first memory of trying squid. "It tastes like pencil erasers, it's good, just try it and spit it out if you don't like it, or you're not going out when Melissa calls for you after dinner" is how I recollect my first experience with scungilli, which most know as conch. For years, I thought mussels in our arms contained black shells underneath. I remember my mother made them for dinner one night in a marinara sauce and I was shocked. I thought we were being asked to eat our biceps! That's when my sister, who is 5 years older, laughed at me and they explained that these were shellfish and that the mussels in our bodies were spelled m-u-s-c-l-e-s. I must have been about 6 years old. I tried them and never looked back.

I suppose the argument can be made that my foodie traits were created by nature, meaning my parents ate these foods, as did their parents, and so on, so that in a Darwinian sense I was genetically predisposed to liking them too? Well then there's the nurture part. The Mother-Daughter house worked out quite well for me growing up. I used it to my advantage. I always had options, plenty of food options. We had what Nana was preparing upstairs and we had what my mother was making downstairs: 2 breakfasts, 2 lunches, and 2 dinners! And the kicker is that it was staggered perfectly. My grandfather was a government worker with regular hours and my Nana had dinner ready when he came home on weeknights, which was about 5-5:30 p.m. My father was a jeweler in Manhattan and worked later so we ended up eating around 7-7:30 p.m. when he got home. It didn't take too long for me to figure out that this was a beautiful thing. I would eat upstairs with Nana and Grandpa, then hit the downstairs menu to eat dinner with my sister and parents a couple of hours later.

None of those eating habits came without consequences, those consequences being from a calorie-conscious, dieting, and figure- conscious mother who laid on the guilt about overeating and laid it on thick. My sister and I went to Catholic school, so we wore uniforms. I can still hear my mom yelling that our skirts were not going to fit anymore and that she had better not have to move the buttons on them. This happened like clockwork every August as we were heading into a new academic year each September. As much as I loved to eat, and had no restrictions from my grandparents upstairs, my mother was always so weight conscious.

It seems like yesterday that I was playing chef, mixing "concoctions" with the creamers, sugar, ketchup and salt and pepper at the diner while my mother's meal order would contain very elaborate instructions with adjectives like "scooped out," "dry," and "no butter," adverbs like "over a bed of lettuce," and nouns like "just the egg whites." I grew up in the mid-late 1970's, early 1980's, the Golden Age of Tab®, Cigarettes, Scarsdale and 3-Day Diets. For years, our refrigerator had a big magnet picture of a pair of eyes that said, "Your Lean Line Lecturer is Watching You." Food, therefore, was always this double-edged sword. Eat - but don't overdo it. As a kid, it always seemed like my mother was on a diet. I can recall my childhood best friend Melissa and I transcribing a diet with crayons on construction paper in the third grade (our backyards were connected, and our moms were best friends too and her mom and my mom would share diets). It would always baffle me how my mother would make such delicious food for my dad and us and then not even eat it.

Being around my mom, Nana Angie and Grandma Susie, I always watched them cook. It's not that they ever sat down and taught me how to cook, it's that I learned to cook. There were no step-by-step explanations, nor was there ever measuring or quantifying. I guess I sort of learned by osmosis and by asking questions. There's a saying that goes, "Italians don't measure seasonings, we just sprinkle and shake until the spirit of our ancestors whisper, 'enough my child.'" I can attest that, in my family, this was totally accurate.

Omnipresent as food was, it even took a role in the way I played as a kid. While many of my friends and girls my age wanted Barbie™ Dolls and play make-up for Christmas, I wanted a hot dog stand, before that the Betty Crocker® Easy Bake Oven and before that the Holly Hobbie™ oven. When Santa actually brought me the hot dog stand that year, I played incessantly with it, flipping burgers, wearing the hat and all. Serving up dogs and fries to family members who would pretend to place orders would make me so happy. I was already earning my stripes in the food service industry. Remember Play Doh? What kid doesn't? We all played with it. When I was a kid, there were only 4 basic colors of Play Doh: red, blue, white and yellow. Many children entertained themselves for hours with the stuff, forming cars, people, or pets. But I'm going to go out on a limb here and say that very few kids played "butcher shop" with the Play Doh. That was my favorite thing to do with it.

We would get the newspaper and a black marker and pretend to shape, wrap and sell all different types of meat or poultry with it, using the bathroom scale, while role-playing with imaginary customers - "Mrs. Mancini, was that 1 pound of chicken cutlets? How would you like those sliced? Thin? Sure. Pounded? Comin' right up!" (enter the yellow Play Doh for chicken) "Mr. McCormack, how are you today? what can I get for you? Center cut pork chops, no problem. They're on sale, $3.99 a pound. How many? 4? Sure thing." (enter the white Play Doh for pork - "the other white meat"). In case you're wondering, beef was red, and veal was blue. Everything was food and food was everything. And we were creative with it.

My sister and I and our friends used to make chocolate molds as kids with my mom - chocolate lollipops were all the rage back in the early 80's, in all different colors and designs. My mom loved to bake as well and, aside from getting scolded for licking the mixer beaters, I loved to be a helper in the kitchen. Christmas baking was epic. My mother and Nana frying up Italian struffoli, rosettes, bows and ribbons with powdered sugar and making Christmas Italian biscotti and American cookies was something we would wait for all year long. My aunts and cousins would come over, to the basement of course, and go to work for hours and hours. Those are some of the best culinary memories I have. Nothing was a chore or done out of obligation. On the contrary, everything was made because we enjoyed it. It was made with passion.

In as much as my mom stayed on top of my sister and me about healthy eating habits (for which I am thankful now), she and my dad also pushed us when it came to our schoolwork and I would not be the person I am today if not for them, in the courtroom or in the kitchen, and my sister would not have been the physician or cook she is either. Although our household was traditional and some would say old-fashioned as my mom was a homemaker, she and my dad made all decisions together. Jointly, they taught us to be independent, respect family, be humble and above all else, have a sense of humor.

We always had part-time jobs, even in high school, and of course, mine centered around food. I worked at a local Italian bakery and a salumeria and also waited tables for a short time. College days were food-filled days as well. I dormed at NYU and naturally, I wanted the comforts of home while there. My father even to this day reminds me that I am the only student in NYU history that has ever stolen their family's red pepper and machinetta (the Italian espresso pot) and taken it to Hayden Hall. What can I say? Guilty as charged but it's not entirely my fault - they're the ones who created this monster.

When I was in college in Manhattan, my sister was in medical school in the Bronx. We would often go home to Staten Island on weekends and my dad would drive us both back Sunday night after dinner, each with cartons and containers of food, including pasta, sauce, meatballs, sausage, chicken, salad, pizza, and foccacia. My roommates would love that I would stock the fridge with such delicious homemade food, and they would put in their orders for the next time. My grandmother still lived in Little Italy at the time and many times on Friday nights I would go eat dinner at her apartment with my dad and sometimes with my roommates.

I am so grateful for my college days living in Greenwich Village, and my law school days at Fordham Law in Manhattan which definitely exposed me to so many different types of cultures and cuisines. It was a real eye-opener having gone from a small, all-girls Catholic high school on the homogenous borough of Staten Island to living with 3 roommates of all different backgrounds across from Washington Square Park in Manhattan. We all hit it off and became friends and bonding over, among other things, the food scene. There are very few things cuisine-wise that Manhattan did not offer. My parents paid for a meal plan for me, but within a few weeks, they quickly learned that I felt that it was not necessary. I would use the meal plan as a supplement, but frequently ordered in from and ate out at Japanese, Chinese, Indian, Greek, and Spanish restaurants.

Fast forward to March 2020. It was not until then that my untapped valuable culinary resources really took center stage. I have no formal culinary training and all of my cooking has been done at home. I always enjoyed cooking, but my life was so consumed with studying, then lawyering and mothering, then, as of recent, becoming a self-employed business owner that I suppose I never seemed to have enough time for it. It was mostly reserved for weekends, holidays, and special occasions. In 2020, that all changed. As days turned into weeks and weeks turned into months and with my livelihood on pause due to the pandemic, and my son learning remotely, I would look at my kitchen, and suddenly feel empowered. Although everything around me was beyond my control, the one thing that was within my control was my daily menu. What began as a creative outlet started to become my daily sustenance, my life support so to speak. Even now, it continues to keep me sane in these uncertain times, feeds my family and allows me to be creative and free. It is with this passion that I was able to write my own "Silver Linings Playbook" and document this journey on how I went from litigation to salivation.

Getting Started

News Flash - great news! You don't need anything overly "cheffy" to make delicious meals. The one essential thing you must have, which cannot be purchased, is PASSION. That is the main ingredient in a good meal and the reason why everything our grandparents and parents made tasted so delicious - they poured their whole heart and soul into the dishes they made. As far as kitchen tools, truth be told, you probably have many of the tools you need in your kitchen cabinets already (if you're anything like me and love to cook, much of your net worth is in kitchenware). Even if you don't do much cooking and are entering unchartered waters, there are a few bells and whistles that you do need, and not only will you feel like a pro using them, but you will likely use them over and over again once you get cooking on the regular.

In addition to plates, bowls, cutlery, and glasses to enjoy your masterpieces, here are some of my top must-have basic tools to have on hand to make things easier, in alphabetical order.

Apron (or whatever your comfortable cooking in that you don't mind getting soiled)
Let's face it, cooking can be a down and dirty business, and some recipes are time-consuming. This isn't the time to hit the nail salon for a new full set of gel tips. Remove your bangles or watch, roll up your sleeves, and put on Sinatra or whatever background music you need to fully immerse yourself into the cooking experience. That's precisely what cooking and baking is, an experience. If you're trying to just "get through" a recipe, I suggest you re-read the second sentence on this page. If your passion isn't there for a particular recipe, then you need to look for a recipe where it is. I promise, it will be worth it.

Baster
You'll want to break this out on more occasions than just Thanksgiving. This is the perfect tool to keep your roasts and chickens juicy and to dip into the meat juices without having to pull out the oven tray. Sometimes you can just use this to easily and safely suction out and dispose of excess liquid from something you are braising stovetop.

Basting brush
Having a couple of food-specific brushes that let you coat foods in oil, sauce or butter with more precision than pouring or spooning, even for egg washes, are always good tools to have.

Blender or food processor
This appliance is essential for soups, pesto, dips, sauces and dressings. I say "or" because many times people only have a blender, and that's fine if it's a good one with sharp blades and you want to "make do," because you have limited space or finance concerns. With a food processor, however, the machine's blade chops or minces foods without forcing too much air inside the food, the way a blender often does. If desired, I would suggest purchasing a simple, yet sturdy food processor with a bowl of at least a 10 cups capacity.

Cake/pie slicer
I can't think of a more terrible thing happening than making an aesthetically pleasing and delicious cake or pie and then it falling apart or smooshing right before your guests' eyes when you go to serve it with a regular bread knife. You want to have your cake and pie presentation be impeccable, and for a small investment in one of these, it will be.

Can opener
I'm Italian. We open sauce cans. Please get a decent one with a sharp blade or you'll be swearing over the music in your kitchen. It doesn't have to be electric or fancy, and with can openers, I find less is more. Same with wine corkscrews. I actually prefer the handheld, old-school ones. If they break, there's no phone call, no product registration or warranty. It can be a beautiful thing.

Cast iron pans

Used to sear, sauté, bake, broil, braise, fry or grill. If possible, I would suggest 2 of these, one 12" and one 15." Lodge Cast Iron is a solid brand and is decently priced. These pans are safe to use in the oven or on the grill and over a fire. They offer unparalleled heat retention and even heating, and you will never taste better steaks or chops than made in a cast-iron pan. They make a perfect frittata, panini, bacon and eggs, crêpes, pan pizza, one-pot pasta, bread puddings, and countless other foods. They are heavy in weight and the handle gets very hot so you should purchase rubber handles for each of them, but I promise you, with the proper cleaning and re-seasoning care, these famously durable pans will be your workhorses and you will have them for years and years to come.

Cheese grater (and/or Microplane/Zester)

You're probably familiar with a traditional box grater, which is a metal four sided object with a top handle that has a different grating surface on each side, from coarse to very fine. This is perfect for all your hard cheeses such as Parmigiano-Reggiano and Pecorino Romano. For finer handheld zesting of citrus fruits, garlic, nutmeg and cinnamon sticks, you may want to invest in a Microplane grater or zester.

Colander - large and small

Some call this a strainer, some, like my family, call it a "scolapasta." The literal translation of this essential culinary tool is "dripping pasta." Some of these are handed down from grandmothers, aunts and others, almost like passing the culinary baton to the younger generation. Don't feel the need to go out and buy a new one - the more beat up, tarnished and dented it is, the more seasoned with love it is and the better it will work! If you don't have one already, invest in one or two of these aluminum gems and it will be a friend for life, and you'll take comfort in the fact that several tons of pasta will pass through those holes.

Cooling rack

This is a wire rack which allows air to circulate freely to cool baked goods and to prevent them from getting soggy from condensation, such as for cookies, scones, muffins, pizzelle, and pizza.

Confectioner's sugar sifter

For baked goods like zeppoles, cakes, pancakes and waffles, you'll want to dust your creations with powdered sugar or cocoa powder. Any fine mesh or strainer can be used for sifting if you don't want to invest in one of these, but they are quite inexpensive and make garnishing the final product fun and easy.

Corer

This tool makes baking apples and apple donuts much easier as the corer glides easily through an apple or pear to remove the core cleanly and seamlessly.

Cutting boards - both wood and plastic

A durable, quality wood cutting board is a smart financial investment and a safe tool. I've heard it said that a cutting board is like a mattress in that if you underestimate the importance of getting a quality one, you will regret it. It should be the primary work surface in your kitchen. When preparing food, especially raw meat, you will want a sturdy reliable surface which is also important in preventing cutting injuries and helps keep your knives from becoming dull too soon. There are advantages to having both wood and plastic in your kitchen.

You should have one well-constructed wood cutting board - at least 1.25" thick, and as large as you can conveniently fit in your kitchen. This will be your workhorse, but you'll need to care for and condition it with food-grade mineral oil to keep it from drying out. I love my John Boos® block.

If feasible, you should probably have a couple of different sized plastic cutting boards as well. The cutting board debate about whether to have wood or plastic still continues. I find having a couple of each to be the most useful. Wood is said to be more antimicrobial than plastic, contrary to popular belief. Plastic has the advantage of being lighter, more inexpensive, space efficient and dishwasher safe. The disadvantage is that they often have to be replaced more often since their surface lends itself to being irreparably scratched by knives and therefore the perfect venue for food-borne bacteria to lie.

The main thing with whatever cutting board you use is be careful of cross-contamination, meaning, if you slice up raw chicken and then use that same board to slice up a cucumber for your salad, you run the risk of the bacteria from the chicken being transferred to the cucumber.

Dish towels & sponges
Some of you may have heard your nonne refer to dish towels as "mappine." Whether you're a cooking Felix (clean as you go) or an Oscar (wait until the very end to clean), you will need a stockpile of these in your kitchen once cooking becomes part of your daily routine, if it isn't already.

Fire extinguisher & baking soda
Safety first. Every kitchen should be equipped with a fire extinguisher and every family member should know where it is and how to use it in case of an emergency. For grease fires, it is good to have a box of baking soda within reach - often we have it in our refrigerator to remove unpleasant odors. Make sure to replace it every few months.

Food scale
Whereas your bathroom scale may not be your friend all the time, your kitchen scale very much will be. If you enjoy baking, it is essential that you have a small digital scale that weighs in both imperial and metric, that gives accurate and consistent measurements, especially if you're working with flour, sugar and salt. For the health conscious, you can also easily measure portion sizes so you can accurately determine calories and other nutritional information per serving.

Garlic press or rocker
For recipes that call for minced or crushed garlic (what Italian recipes don't?), this tool is perfect. It crushes quickly, efficiently, and evenly, and you don't have to worry about the smell of garlic on your fingers.

Hand juicer
If your recipe calls for a small amount of juice, usually a lemon, lime or orange, using this small handheld press tool is much easier than a juicer.

Herb mill
I'm a self-admitted fresh herbs snob. I suspect that once you start cooking with fresh herbs, and their aroma permeates your kitchen and dining table, you will never go back to the dried herbs again. Mince parsley, dill, mint, cilantro, basil and sage with this handheld device and it will soon be your best friend. Your guests will think they're dining at a 5-star restaurant with your garnishing abilities.

Honey drizzler
Also known as a honey dipper or honey wand, I love having this to drizzle honey in tea, on cereal, oats, pancakes, waffles, buns, yogurts and dessert. If used correctly, it's much less messy than using a spoon and it does not drip sticky honey onto the rim or jar like a spoon does. They are also useful for other thick and sticky items like syrups, melted chocolate and caramel sauce.

Hot plates
Also known as trivets, several of these are essential in serving hot food family style to prevent burning your countertop, table or tablecloth.

Immersion blender
This is also known as a hand blender, handheld blender, or stick blender. Nowadays usually cordless, you place it into a pot or container of liquid to blend ingredients, such as for soups, smoothies and purées. It's safer than transferring scalding liquid into a blender. Some come with certain attachments like a whisk, mini chopper, milk frother, or potato masher so you can actually start and end in the same bowl - one less dish to wash is always a plus! You want to look for one that is comfortable to hold and operate with one hand, is easy to clean, and has a pan guard to protect your cookware.

Knives (chef's, bread, utility, paring, cleaver, kitchen shears, steak knives, carving knives & sharpening tool)

If there is one item in the kitchen that you will get the biggest return on your investment, it is a quality set of kitchen knives and a sharpening tool or stone. Walking into the knives section at a store like Williams-Sonoma can be daunting and rest assured you don't need every knife in a manufacturer's collection. You should however, have a chef's knife (curved to allow the cook to rock the knife on the cutting board for a more precise cut), a carving knife, a bread knife, which is serrated or perforated, a paring knife for fruits and vegetables, a meat cleaver, and a utility knife (between a chef's and paring knife in size), sharp kitchen shears or scissors for cutting meats and poultry, cleaning shrimp, prepping kale and other greens, slicing pizza, among other things, and a decent set of steak knives for the table.

Ladle

Also known by Italians as a "mestolo," this is a deep spoon with a long handle used for serving sauces, stews, soups and punch. You really can get by with only one of these, and the larger volume capacity the better, 8 ounces or more.

Mallet

You want to have one of these handy to pound chicken, veal or pork cutlets and tenderize your steaks in preparation for cooking, with cuts such as flank or skirt steak.

Measuring cups and spoons, pourable

For ease of pouring measured liquid, I suggest pourable measuring cups and spoons. Although we often are used to sometimes "eyeballing" ingredients, for new recipes it is important to measure exact quantities.

Mezzaluna

A mezzaluna is a thin slicing knife with one or more curved blades (mezzaluna means "half-moon" shape in Italian) and with handles on each end, which is rocked back and forth in order to evenly and consistently slice and chop ingredients. Ideal for home cooks who do not have the luxury of having a collection of quality knives, a mezzalua can be used to prepare a soffritto (carrots, celery and onions) as well as to chop basil for pesto, and other herbs and garlic. In fact, a large, single-blade sharp mezzaluna is my go-to for cutting my pizza. You can invest in a traditional round, single-hand pizza cutter but make sure it's a sharp one, as many of the ones on the market are dull and don't give you defined cuts.

Mixer

As much as I love a stunningly functional Kitchen Aid® Stand Mixer, I cannot, in good conscience, advise you to spend all kinds of money on one when the fact is that you could use a hand mixer for any of my recipes in this book. If you have one, great. If not, you can easily get by with a quality hand mixer for these recipes. Nowadays, the hand mixers are up to 9 speeds, many are even cordless, with various attachments. On the contrary, if you're regularly making pizza dough, bread and pasta, then investing in a stand mixer with dough hook, paddle and various other attachments would definitely make more sense.

Mixing bowls

You will want to have varying sizes of mixing bowls, be they glass or plastic, for all your cooking and baking recipes.

Muddler

To make an amazing cocktail you will want one of these for smashing fruits on the bottom of a glass and to release the oils in herbs like mint. A muddler also comes in handy for crushing nuts or mashing small food like avocados.

Muffin tins

Chances are you may already have these and, in addition to their stated purpose, they will come in handy for egg bites, mini tacos and breakfast quesadillas.

Non-stick skillet pans

Also known as frying pans, you'll want a couple of these shallow frying pans on hand, either stainless steel or aluminum, for several of my recipes in this cookbook.

Oven mitts
You will be handling hot items in and out of the oven and these are much safer, easier and more sanitary than using dish cloths.

Parchment paper & wax paper
Essential to line baking pans, this moisture and grease-resistant paper will be useful from oven-roasting meats to baking cookies, effectively freezing meats and everything in between. You will save tons of time on clean-up and save your pans at the same time.

Pasta scooper
This is also known as a pasta fork and it's not to be confused with a pasta spoon, which you should also have, that has several holes or slots, allowing you to test for pasta readiness, this scooper is mainly for serving long pastas such as linguine, spaghetti, long fusilli, and bucatini. At the same time it also helps grip pasta through a center slot and drains any excess water from the cooked pasta.

Pizza cutter
See Mezzaluna above

Pizza pans
For pan pizzas such as Sicilians, Detroit Style and Grandma pizzas made in your conventional oven you will want to get some anodized aluminum pre-seasoned pans such as Lloyd Pans®, which are rust-resistant and scratch proof.

Pizza peel
If you're making a good deal of pizza at home, you will want to invest in a sturdy wooden pizza peel to launch your pizza, as well as metal turning peel in order to rotate it or get it close to the broiler. These will also be useful if you have an outdoor pizza oven.

Pizza stone or steel
If you want to make a quality pizza at home, you will need to purchase one of these. A preheated stone or steel absorbs and retains heat which is transferred to the pizza undercarriage and crust. I highly recommend a Baking Steel® - it was a total game changer for my pizzas.

Pizzelle iron
If there is one splurge purchase on this list, it's a pizzelle iron, and you can get a good one for less than $50. This is an electric iron used to make pizzelle, which is a delicious Italian cookie, traditionally made around Christmas. You can also use the iron to make cannoli shells or waffles and it will become your holiday staple.

Potato masher
Not just a one-hit wonder for mashing potatoes, this kitchen tool will come in handy anytime you desire that nice chunky consistency, for example, for crushing whole tomatoes, bananas, avocados, apple sauce or refried beans.

Potato ricer
This is a kitchen tool for making the perfect fluffy mashed potatoes or to process potatoes for homemade gnocchi or in a soup. I like the Oxo brand potato ricer.

Ramekins
These adorable and versatile containers will be practical for cooking and serving individual portions of soups, baked apples, and dips.

Rolling pin
Every baker has a favorite rolling pin, whether it's one they inherited from a family member or one they bought themselves. I prefer a marble to a wood rolling pin, not because it's called a French rolling pin or because I want to be fancy. First, marble conducts heat away from the dough quicker than wood and I find the dough gets much less sticky. They are especially good for cool-sensitive doughs like puff pastry. Thus, they are easier to clean since there are no nooks where dough and flour can hide. Lastly, they are very heavy so they can help flatten a stiff dough with ease by their weight. However, the only downside is if it falls, it is likely to cause much more damage than its wooden counterpart.

Salt and pepper mill

If you want to elevate ho-hum cooking to the realm of flavorful gourmet meals with fresher and fuller flavor, definitely invest in a good salt and pepper mill. They will go a long way into your cooking future. It's how you'll want your savory dishes to taste. The mills keep the spices potent and fresh until you're ready to use them so you grind as you go. Once these spices are ground, they begin to oxidize and lose their potency, which means you'll have to use more spices to get the same effect, potentially saving you money and protecting your cooking from stale spices. It's best to purchase and fill your own mills as opposed to the pre-filled type you see in the stores since the mechanism itself may be inferior, you don't know how fresh that salt and those peppercorns are inside.

Sauté pan

Like skillets or frying pans, a sauté pan can be used to cook on the stovetop. Unlike a frying pan, a sauté pan is usually much deeper. The pan's straight vertical sides are designed to hold a greater volume and prevent spills. Slow-cooking recipes that contain lots of liquid broths or sauces will benefit from the depth and large, flat cooking surface of a sauté pan.

Spatula - rubber and metal

A rubber spatula is necessary for scraping every last drop of the sticky contents inside of bowls, canned foods, food processors or blenders, such as for batters, soups, sauces and pesto. You may benefit from rubber spatulas of different sizes. I sometimes use these to smear chocolate or frosting while baking as well.

A good metal spatula is an essential component of any cook's kit. Sometimes referred to as a turner or flipper, it is a broad, flat utensil used to flip or transfer foods such as burgers, patties, or pancakes when you are cooking with metal cook or bakeware. When using cast iron cookware, you may also want to invest in a silicone spatula since the soft material will not cause any damage to the cooking surface area.

Spray misters (for olive oil, etc.)

I have a few bottles of these and find them particularly useful for different oils, extracts, vinegar and even soy sauce. They are perfect for evenly coating salads, chicken, barbecuing and even baking when you want to control the amount of what's being sprayed. Misting oil is safe for use on non-stick skillets and healthier to use than aerosol spray oils. It is also great for re-seasoning your cast iron pans.

Splatter screen

Splatter screens are usually made of metal and mesh with a long handle (I prefer the handle be made of silicone) to catch the droplets of grease that fly out of the pan when meat or vegetables hit the hot pan while you are cooking stovetop. Not only do these make cooking safer and prevent burns, but they make cleanup of your stove a whole lot easier. You really only need one of these which should be large enough to cover the diameter of your largest pan. It does not matter that it will overlap your smaller ones.

Stock pots, saucepans, and sheet pans

It is a good idea to have these in various sizes depending on how many people for whom you are cooking. An enamel coated Dutch oven in either a 5 quart or 7 quart capacity is always a good investment. You don't need to spend a fortune on cookware. I like All-Clad® Metalcasters and Le Creuset® brands. That said, make sure your pots have thick and durable bottoms. Stainless steel or aluminum pans are always a good choice. There are pros and cons to both materials. Aluminum is popular as it is inexpensive and conducts heat quickly and well. Stainless steel is scratch-resistant, corrosion-resistant and non-reactive. It is durable and oven-safe, but usually has to be hand-washed. You could also find a stainless steel cookware set with an aluminum core to get the best of both worlds.

Taster(s)

Ideally, you will want tasters who are tactfully honest to sample your cooking and baking in the event you need to improve on recipes, which can sometimes be a work in progress. You may prefer more salt or pepper or spice than I (highly doubt that!), and that is where tasters come in, especially if they are family members or friends with whom you will be dining regularly.

Thermometer - oven thermometer and meat thermometer

It's surely a pro move to make sure your oven is the correct temperature. This is a thermometer you manually place inside the oven. You may be surprised when you use a thermometer to discover that your oven is not actually performing at the temperature that it is set to.

A meat thermometer is usually one with a long straight probe with a round needle dial or digital display that sits on top. It is essential to have so you won't have to engage in "guesswork" to determine whether your chicken, turkey, pork, beef or lamb is sufficiently cooked.

Tin foil
What else can I say that you don't already know about this magnificent invention? You can never have enough tin foil to wrap up leftovers, cover meats in the oven, barbeque fish and vegetables and line baking pans.

Tongs
Having one large set and one small set of tongs is a good idea. These are used to grip, maneuver and flip foods while cooking in the oven or on the stovetop, or transferring fried foods from one place to another, like a paper towel, such as in the case of chicken cutlets, meatballs, and zeppole.

Toothpicks
Self-explanatory, but they often come in handy for testing baked cakes, for cherries and garnishes on cocktails, for ham glazing, roasting baked potatoes, grabbing cheese or olives on a platter, or for holding together wraps and sandwiches.

Tupperware®
If you are anything like me, you will cook for a small army and will relish leftovers, to be either refrigerated or frozen. You will want to invest in several assorted size containers with lids. Quart or pint size take-out food containers are perfect for soup or sauce storage, so don't be so quick to dispose of those!

Vegetable peeler
This is ideal for prepping tough-skinned fruits and vegetables, like potatoes, carrots, apples and pears.

Whisks
Having a few of these of different sizes in your arsenal will be needed for making eggs, batter, creams and sauces.

Wine
Grab a glass of vino to enjoy while you're cooking (if you're over 21) and it's certain to be a more relaxing and fun experience. Red or white wine is also called for as an ingredient in certain recipes which makes it a win-win (although many times the wines we drink may be too high quality to put in a dish when it's going to burn off).

Wooden spoons
This is not just a domestic weapon in Italian households, it actually is a very useful kitchen tool. Haha! I have several of these in my collection, and they are my go-to for stirring sauces, including Sunday Sauce, as well as using the flat edged one to scrape up the bits on the bottom of the sauté pan. The beauty about wood is that it is not a heat conductor, whereas metal is, so you can leave it in the pot for a minute or two while tending to other immediate tasks and you won't run the risk of burning your hand. I also love a lazy wooden spoon that has a little notch enabling it to hook onto the pot you're using so you won't misplace it when you're running around your kitchen multitasking.

Your phone/Ipad/computer with Internet
This is essential since if you don't understand a recipe, you can easily go online and search images or quick presentation videos. Chances are, you'll find something similar, or you can always shoot me an e-mail and I'd be happy to help. Additionally, you may be unable to find a certain ingredient or cooking tool in the store, so can easily order those online (so you'll need a credit card too!). Certainly not least, you're going to need to memorialize your beautiful culinary masterpieces so you'll need your phone, ipad or computer camera to snap some shots for bragging rights!

This list is definitely not exhaustive but is merely a guide so that you can comfortably make all the recipes in this cookbook and hopefully more in the future. For example, I consider a lasagna pan and molcajete necessary, but since this cookbook does not contain a lasagna or guacamole recipe, I did not mention it. And lastly, if and when you can creatively substitute one kitchen tool for another that is not accessible to you, go right ahead! I welcome creativity and ingenuity inside and outside of the kitchen. Happy cooking!

Ingredients matter. Freshness matters more. Hand-grown matters most.

*The more colorful the food the better -
variety is certainly the spice of life.*

Breakfast & Brunch

Savory Pesto Waffles

Hold the maple syrup and pass the pesto. There is nothing like putting a spin on traditional waffles with a recipe that turns breakfast into brunch and brunch into dinner and back again. These are probably the most delicious fluffy, savory waffles you will ever eat. Create a fresh and fragrant basil pesto* to use in the batter, spread on top and be sure to keep some leftover sauce in the freezer for next time. And trust me, there will be a next time.

*Using the Pesto Alla Genovese recipe for homemade pesto (page 67).

SERVINGS: 4 large waffles | Prep Time: 5 minutes | Cooking Time: 15 minutes

INGREDIENTS:
2 1/4 cups of all purpose flour
1 1/3 cups of milk
1 tablespoon of baking powder
1 whole egg
1 tablespoon of grated Parmigiano-Reggiano cheese, plus more for garnish
2 tablespoons of vegetable oil
4 tablespoons of homemade pesto plus more for drizzling

DIRECTIONS:
1. Stir ingredients until blended.

2. Pour onto center of a hot greased waffle maker. Close lid.

3. Bake about 5 minutes or until steaming stops or light on your iron goes on/off.

4. Carefully remove waffles.

5. Drizzle with extra pesto sauce. Serve with grated Parmigiano-Reggiano and sliced tomatoes, if desired.

Pecan Praline Scones with Maple Glaze

I definitely have a thing for homemade scones, especially glazed ones. These are topped with a creamy maple glaze and a sprinkle of pecans. Enjoy one with your favorite latte, coffee or cup of hot tea. They're a delicious treat any time of day.

SERVINGS: 8 | Prep Time: 20 minutes | Cooking Time: 15 minutes

INGREDIENTS:

For the scones:
2 cups of all-purpose flour
1/3 cup of brown sugar
1 tablespoon of baking powder
1/2 teaspoon of salt
1/2 cup of cold butter, cut into 1/2-inch cubes
1 cup of whipping cream, divided
1/4 cup of chopped pralines
1/4 cup of chopped pecans
Wax paper

For the maple glaze:
1/4 tablespoons of maple syrup
2 tablespoons of very soft butter
2-3 tablespoons of heavy cream
2 tablespoons of dark brown sugar
1/4 cup of cinnamon
1 cup of confectioners' sugar, or more if needed
1 teaspoon of vanilla extract

DIRECTIONS:

1. Preheat oven to 450°F. Stir together the flour, sugar, baking powder and salt in a large bowl. Cut the butter into the flour mixture with a hand mixer until crumbly and the mixture resembles small peas. Freeze for 5 minutes. Add 3/4 cup plus 2 tablespoons of cream and the pralines and pecans, stirring just until the dry ingredients are moistened.

2. Empty the dough onto wax paper. Gently knead or pat the dough into a circle with about a 7" diameter - the mixture will seem crumbly. Cut the round into 8 equally sized wedges or use a scone pan. Place the wedges on a lightly greased baking sheet a few inches apart from each other. Brush the tops of the wedges with the remaining 2 tablespoons of cream just until moistened.

3. Bake at 450°F for 13-15 minutes or until golden. Let the scones cool before icing them.

4. While the scones are baking, make the maple glaze. Place the maple syrup, cream, butter, brown sugar and cinnamon in a medium size microwave safe bowl. Cook on high power for about 1 minute. Whisk well to smooth out any lumps. Cook for another minute until the mixture is vigorously bubbling.

5. Remove the glaze from the microwave and add powdered sugar and vanilla to make a thick but drizzle-able glaze. If it seems too thin, thicken it by adding more confectioners' sugar and if the mixture seems too thick, add a little more cream to liquify it.

6. Drizzle the glaze over the scones. Let them sit for about 15 minutes to let the glaze set before serving.

Lemon Ricotta Pancakes

You'll never regret having a unique pancake recipe in your arsenal. There are so many delicious recipes out there, but this one will give you light fluffy, lemony cakes that are not too dense and are great-tasting, without the need for lots of heavy toppings. You can, of course add some to jazz them up, but made correctly, with a little sprinkle of confectioners' sugar and some fresh berries, these will be the star of your breakfast show all by themselves.

SERVINGS: 4-6 small pancakes | Prep Time: 10 minutes | Cooking Time: 20 minutes

INGREDIENTS:

4 large eggs, separated
1/3 cup plus 1 tablespoon of sugar, divided
1 cup of all-purpose flour
1 teaspoon of baking powder
1/2 teaspoon of salt plus 1 pinch for beating the egg whites
1 cup of whole milk ricotta
1/4 teaspoon of vanilla extract
3 tablespoons of fresh-squeezed lemon juice
2 teaspoons of lemon zest
1/2 cup of whole or 2% milk
Butter or vegetable oil for the griddle or pan
Fresh blueberries to serve
Maple syrup to serve
Confectioners' sugar to serve

DIRECTIONS:

1. Separate the eggs and carefully place the whites and yolks in separate bowls.

2. Beat the egg whites in a mixer bowl with a pinch of salt at high speed until they are frothy then add 1 tablespoon of sugar slowly. Continue beating until the eggs form stiff peaks, about 4-5 minutes and set aside.

3. Combine the dry ingredients together in a bowl, whisking the flour, baking powder and 1/2 teaspoon of the salt until blended. Set aside.

4. In a large bowl, whisk the egg yolks and remaining 1/3 cup of sugar. Add the ricotta, lemon juice, lemon zest, and vanilla extract and whisk until smooth. Stir in the milk until blended.

5. Add the flour mixture to the egg yolk mixture and stir with a spatula. Fold in 1/3 of the beaten egg white to lighten the batter, then add the remaining egg whites until only a few streaks of white remain.

6. Brush a cast iron pan, non-stick skillet or griddle with oil or butter over medium-low heat. After heat checking (usually a flick of water sizzling on contact), scoop the batter and drop into the pan, spreading each with a spoon to form about a 4-5" round pancake.

7. Cook each pancake for about 1-2 minutes or until bubbles form and then flip to other side, cooking for 1-2 minutes longer if necessary, until the pancakes are cooked through, always on medium-low heat, careful not to burn them.

Zucchini Bread

A perennial favorite, I love making this bread when the garden is overflowing with this summer vegetable. This easy bread, which my mom always used to make us as kids, is an old fashioned, moist and gently spiced favorite.

SERVINGS: 12 slices | Prep Time: 15 minutes | Cooking Time: 50-55 minutes

INGREDIENTS:
1 1/2 cups of grated zucchini - lightly packed, do not drain liquid
1 1/2 cups of all-purpose flour
1 cup of granulated sugar
1/4 cup of lightly packed brown sugar
1/2 cup of vegetable oil
1/2 cup of unsweetened applesauce
2 large eggs
1 teaspoon of vanilla extract
1/2 teaspoon of baking powder
1/2 teaspoon of baking soda
1/2 teaspoon of salt
1/2 teaspoon of ground cinnamon
1/4 teaspoon of ground nutmeg
1/3 cup of chopped walnuts (if desired)
1/3 cup of raisins (if desired)

DIRECTIONS:
1. Preheat oven to 350°F. Spray a 9x5 inch loaf pan with cooking spray.

2. In a large bowl, add the grated zucchini, sugar, brown sugar, eggs, oil, and vanilla. Whisk until well combined.

3. Add the flour, baking powder, baking soda, salt, cinnamon, nutmeg, nuts and raisins. Stir until no dry flour remains, careful not to over mix.

4. Pour the batter into the loaf pan. Bake for 50 to 55 minutes. Insert a toothpick into the center of the bread and if it comes out clean with moist crumbs on it, the bread is done.

5. Cool in the pan for 10 minutes. Remove the pan and transfer to a cooling rack to cool completely before slicing.

6. Store covered in the refrigerator the bread is best served after it has been refrigerated for at least 12 hours.

Muffin Pan Southwest Egg Bites

These were my go-to breakfast before busy on-the-go mornings in court and for my son on school mornings. They're the perfect easy addition to any weekly a.m. meal routine. On weekends, when there's more time, you can even add some extra shredded cheese, tortilla chips and salsa for a nacho flair! If you have time, making a double batch is ideal. Save some for breakfast and freeze the rest as you plan for a busy week.

SERVINGS: 12 standard size muffin egg bites | Prep Time: 10 minutes | Cooking Time: 15-20 minutes

INGREDIENTS:
1 cup of black beans, drained
7 jumbo eggs
3 scallions, chopped
1/4 cup of red onion, minced
3/4 cup of shredded cheddar cheese
1/2 cup of combined diced red, green and yellow peppers
2 tablespoons of milk
Salt and pepper, to taste
Vegetable oil to coat the pan
1 sliced jalapeño pepper, if desired on the side
Sour cream and salsa, if desired on the side

DIRECTIONS:
1. Preheat oven to 350°F.

2. In a large bowl, beat the eggs, cheese, milk, onions, scallions and peppers, salt and pepper. Grease the insides and sides of muffin pan with either a spray vegetable or use a paper towel.

3. Spoon about 1 tablespoon of drained black beans into each muffin slot.

4. Pour the egg mixture on top of each, careful not to fill all the way to the top (as these rise).

5. Sprinkle a couple of peppers and some more cheese at the top. Bake for about 15-20 minutes or until the center is still slightly jiggly. Cool on a rack and serve. If they are stubborn in coming out, use a butter knife along the perimeter of the egg bite and wedge them out.

Crêpes with Strawberry and Blueberry Compote

Viva la crêpe! If you want to really wow your guests with a brunch crowd-pleaser, make crêpes. They are so versatile in that they could be made sweet or savory. I like to think of crêpes as a blank canvas. Delicious fresh fruit compotes work so well as a filling because you can use them for so many different things as well - like cakes, ice cream, yogurts, or cheese and crackers.

✗

SERVINGS: 10-12 large crêpes | Prep Time: 40 minutes | Cooking Time: 30 minutes

INGREDIENTS:

2 jumbo room temperature eggs
1 tablespoon of granulated sugar
1 1/2 teaspoon of vanilla extract
3 tablespoons of unsalted butter plus 4 tablespoons additional for the pan
3/4 cup of 2% or whole milk at room temperature (for richer tasing you may use half & half or cream but not anything lower fat than 2%)

1/8 teaspoon of salt
1 cup of all-purpose flour
1/2 cup of water at room temperature

DIRECTIONS:

1. Heat 3 tablespoons of butter on the stove or in the microwave. Let it cool for a few minutes.
2. Combine the cooled melted butter, eggs, flour, sugar, salt, milk, and water in a medium size mixing bowl (to either whisk or use a hand mixer) or a blender. Blend on medium for about 30 seconds (or whisk) until everything is combined. The mixture should be silky smooth and have a creamy consistency. Cover the blender (or bowl) tightly and chill in the refrigerator for at least 30 to 60 minutes and up to one day.
3. The rest of the butter is for greasing in the pan after each crêpe. Please an 8" nonstick skillet on medium heat and generously grease it with some butter. You can use a larger skillet if you don't have one this size but be sure to make the crêpes thin. When the skillet is hot, pour about 3 tablespoons of batter into the center of the pan. Twirl or tilt the pan in a circular motion so the batter stretches as far as it can go. The thinner the crêpe the better the texture - otherwise it will end up tasting like a pancake. Cook for 1 to 2 minutes then flip as soon as the bottom is set.
4. Transfer the cooked crêpe onto a large plate lined with parchment paper and repeat this step with the remaining batter, making sure that you butter the pan in between each crêpe. Layer the crêpes with parchment paper to prevent them sticking to each other. This also helps keep them warm. If you are generous with the butter, however, they really should not stick together. If the ones you made previously became too cool, then place a moistened damp paper towel over the plate of crêpes and microwave for 30 seconds (if you have a tortilla warmer this is ideal as well). Putting them in the oven will dry them out.
5. You can fill the crêpes with your favorite filling or serve with toppings. They are ideal warm but may be served at room temperature as well. If you are filling them, carefully place filling in the center of the crêpe and fold both sides over the filling.*These crêpes can be made with sweet or savory toppings/fillings. For savory, you can eliminate the vanilla and substitute any number of items: black pepper, cayenne pepper, spices or grated cheese to the batter.
6. To store leftover (unfilled) crêpes, place them in an airtight container in the refrigerator for 1 day or freezer for 1 month using parchment paper in between the layers of crêpes in a freezer zipper bag. Thaw at room temperature before enjoying them.

Strawberry & Blueberry Compote:
SERVINGS: 8 | Prep Time: 5 minutes | Cooking Time: 10 minutes

INGREDIENTS:

1 pound of sliced strawberries or whole blueberries (you may use frozen)
3 tablespoons of lemon juice

2 tablespoons of granulated sugar
2 tablespoons of cornstarch

DIRECTIONS:

1. Place the berries in a saucepan. Add the sugar and juice or water. Bring to a boil. Reduce the heat to low and simmer until the strawberries or blueberries are all soft and just starting to fall apart and the liquid thickens, between 5 to 10 minutes.
2. Taste and add more sugar if necessary. The compote will thicken a little while it cools off, but if it seems too thin, mix 1 tablespoon of water with 1 tablespoon of cornstarch and add it to the saucepan. If using frozen strawberries or blueberries you might need a little more cornstarch. Stir well and remove from heat.
3. Let the compote cool off completely. Transfer to a clean airtight glass pint jar and store in the refrigerator for up to 2 weeks.

You can also play around with the flavors and add a berry liquor or wine, since the alcohol evaporates during cooking, leaving just the flavor behind or add a flavored balsamic vinegar for a tangy edge, or even slice up some hot chili, jalapeño or habanero peppers to give the compote a kick. The final product should be much looser than the consistency of a jam (even though the cooking process is similar) and contain chunks of fruit for topping.

Lemon Blueberry Loaf

From the moment I stepped foot on the island of Capri, I realized that lemons are my love language. This amazing lemony bread always reminds me of the dwindling days of summer and it's something that I've made for my son, unglazed, as a delicious send-off for the perfect on-the-go, back to school breakfast. Topped with a tangy and sweet lemon glaze, this anytime bread-turned-dessert is sure be a showstopper.

SERVINGS: 1 loaf | Prep Time: 15 minutes | Cooking Time: 60-70 minutes

INGREDIENTS:
1 1/2 cups of all-purpose flour
1/3 cup of melted butter or vegetable spread
1/2 teaspoon of salt
1 cup of fresh or frozen blueberries
2 tablespoons of blueberry balsamic
1/2 cup of milk (2% or whole)
1/2 cup of chopped walnuts
2 tablespoons of grated lemon zest
1 teaspoon of baking powder
1 cup of sugar
3 tablespoons of fresh squeezed lemon juice
2 large eggs at room temperature

For the glaze:
3 tablespoons of lemon juice
3/4 cup of confectioners' sugar

DIRECTIONS:
1. Preheat oven to 350°F. Mix together the melted butter, sugar, lemon juice and eggs in a large bowl followed by the flour, baking powder and salt. Then stir the milk into the egg mixture while whisking. Fold in the walnuts, lemon zest and blueberries last.

2. Transfer all ingredients to a greased loaf pan approximately 8" x 4." Bake at 350°F for about 60 minutes until a toothpick in center comes out clean. Cool about 10 minutes before transferring to a wire rack.

3. Mix together the glaze ingredients until completely smooth and drizzle over the warm loaf. Let it cool completely.

Appetizers

Caponatina

Each time I make this delicious dish over the summer, it always seems that no matter how much I make, it's never enough as my family and friends all want their own jar. The pleasant sweet and sour aroma fills the house for days. Caponata or Caponatina (the -ina at the end of the word implies small or cute, as in finely chopped caponata) is at the cornerstone of Sicilian agrodolce cooking. It is basically the sweet and sour version of ratatouille. Because eggplant absorbs flavors like a sponge, it's particularly good in such a pungent dish. Like most eggplant dishes, this gets better overnight. It's meant to be served at room temperature, and it is delicious cold as well. It makes a great topping for homemade bruschetta.

SERVINGS: 6 | Prep Time: 30 minutes (additional time if you salt eggplant and let it sit in a colander for 20 minutes to sweat out the bitterness) | Cooking Time: 40-50 minutes

INGREDIENTS:

5-6 tablespoons of extra virgin olive oil
Vegetable oil, for sautéing eggplant
Fine sea salt and black pepper, to taste
1/4 cup of toasted pignoli nuts
2 cloves of minced garlic
1/4 cup of capers, rinsed and drained
1/2 cup of tomato paste
1/2 cup of water
2 tablespoons of sugar
3 ribs of celery, cut into 1/2-inch dice
1 large eggplant, peeled, alternating with 1-inch strips of skin retained and diced into 1-inch cubes

1/2 pound of pitted Castelvetrano olives
1/2 pound of black oil-cured olives
1 red bell pepper, cored and chopped
1 cup of fresh cherry tomatoes, chopped
1/4 cup of red or golden raisins
Pinch of red pepper
3 tablespoons of red wine vinegar
1 medium white onion, cubed
Fresh basil leaves, for garnish
Fresh chopped parsley, for garnish

* You can adjust to find your desired balance of tangy-sweet-salty-spicy. Add more or less vinegar, raisins, sugar, red pepper flakes or salt.

DIRECTIONS:

1. Preheat oven to 400°F. After cutting the eggplant, salting it and allowing it to sit in a colander for about 20 minutes to sweat out the bitterness (this is optional), pat it dry with a paper towel. Coat the bottom of a large skillet with vegetable oil. When glistening, sauté the eggplant until it is browned. When finished, spread it on a large sheet pan. Drizzle with about 2-3 tablespoons of olive oil and roast in the oven for about 25-30 minutes until it is fully cooked and tender.

2. Heat 3 tablespoons of olive oil in a large skillet. Add the onions, celery, garlic, and bell pepper. Season with a pinch of sea salt and black pepper. Cook for about 5-7 minutes, tossing until tender.

3. Add the sugar and vinegar to a small saucepan over low heat, stirring until fully dissolved.

4. Add the tomato paste, tomatoes, capers, raisins, olives, crushed red pepper and water to the large skillet with the celery, bell pepper, onion and garlic mixture and stir to combine, along with the sugar and vinegar mixture from the small saucepan. Simmer on medium-low heat for about 10 minutes.

5. Stir in the roasted eggplant and cook for another 2-3 minutes in the sauce. Finish with previously toasted pignoli nuts, parsley and fresh basil. For best results, let sit at room temperature for about 1 hour before serving or store in the refrigerator overnight and serve cold or at room temperature with crostini or toasted ciabatta bread.

Bread Bowl Spinach Artichoke Dip

The only thing better than spinach and artichoke dip is warm spinach and artichoke dip in a bread bowl. This easy, cheesy crowd-pleasing recipe comes together in 30 minutes and is one of my go-to recipes for entertaining or bringing over to someone's home for game day. Even the little ones have fun breaking off pieces of bread and dipping!

✕

SERVINGS: 6-8 | Prep Time: 5 minutes | Cooking Time: 15-20 minutes

INGREDIENTS:
1 peasant or round sourdough bread
3 tablespoons of extra virgin olive oil
3 cloves of garlic, minced
1/2 teaspoon of red pepper flakes
1 cup of fresh or frozen spinach (thawed and drained)
1 14-ounce can of artichoke hearts, chopped
8 ounces of room temperature cream cheese
1 cup of sour cream or 2% Greek yogurt
1 cup of shredded mozzarella cheese, divided
3/4 cup of grated Parmigiano-Reggiano cheese
1/4 cup of Pecorino Romano cheese
Salt and pepper, to taste

DIRECTIONS:
1. In a saucepan over medium heat, add 2 tablespoons of olive oil, garlic and red pepper for about 30 seconds until garlic is fragrant.

2. Stir in spinach, artichokes, cream cheese, sour cream, half of the mozzarella, Parmigiano-Reggiano, and Pecorino Romano cheese. Stir until the cheese is melted.

3. Season with salt and pepper, remove from heat and set aside.

4. Preheat oven to 375°F. Remove the top of the bread, with a sharp knife, cut around the inside of the bread, careful not to pierce through the sides, and scoop out the center.

5. Cut the scooped-out bread into cubes and place them on a baking sheet lined with parchment paper. Mist or drizzle the cube bread pieces with the remaining 1 tablespoon of olive oil.

6. If you choose, you may slice into the edges of the bread bowl cutting all the way through the bottom leaving about 1 inch of space between each. Place onto a baking sheet.

7. Spoon in the spinach artichoke mixture into the hollowed-out bread and sprinkle the remaining mozzarella along the edges of the top of the filled bread bowl.

8. Place the sliced top back onto the bowl and bake both the filled bowl and bread cubes for 15-20 minutes. You may broil to the bowl for a couple of minutes at the end to crisp the cheese. Serve and enjoy!

Cherry Cola Chicken Wings

These wings are equally crispy, sticky, sweet with just enough kick for all to enjoy. If your family and friends are always rooting for a sports team no matter what and you need a dish to fill their tummies, or if you really want to wow your guests for a backyard BBQ this will be your go-to wing recipe.

✕

SERVINGS: 4 | Prep Time: 15 minutes | Cooking Time: 35 minutes

INGREDIENTS:
2 1/2 pounds of chicken wings separated into drumettes and wing pieces
3 tablespoons of vegetable oil
1 tablespoon of kosher salt
1/2 teaspoon of black pepper

For the sauce:
2 tablespoons of vegetable oil
1 red onion, chopped about 1 1/2cups
2 garlic cloves, grated
2 chopped jalapeños
1/2 teaspoon of kosher salt
1/2 teaspoon of garlic powder
1/4 teaspoon of dry mustard
1/4 teaspoon of black pepper
2 cups of cherry cola
1/2 cup of red wine vinegar
1/2 teaspoon of smoked paprika
1 cup of ketchup

DIRECTIONS:
1. Position in oven rack in the top third of the oven. Preheat the oven to 450°F. Line a baking sheet with foil.

2. Place the chicken wings on a prepared baking sheet. Toss with 3 tablespoons of oil, 1 tablespoon of the salt and 1/2 teaspoon of the black pepper. Bake until the wings are completely cooked through and just beginning to brown, about 25 minutes. Open the oven and flip the wings over onto the other side and cook another 5 minutes.

3. While the chicken wings bake, prepare the barbecue sauce. Heat the vegetable oil in a saucepan over medium heat. Add the red onions and cook until translucent. Add the garlic and jalapeño, cooking an additional minute. Add the garlic powder, smoked paprika, salt, mustard powder, and black pepper. Toss the spices until fragrant and deep maroon in color, about one minute. Star in the cherry soda, red wine vinegar and ketchup until combined. Bring to a boil and cook until the sauce has thickened and reduced about 10 minutes. Remove from the heat and let cool slightly and then purée in a blender until smooth. Extra sauce can be kept in the refrigerator for up to one week or frozen for the next time around.

4. When the wings are cooked through and beginning to brown, remove the baking sheet and turn the oven to broil setting. Pour the sauce over the wings, toss to coat and then put them back on to the broiler until they are crisp about 2 to 3 minutes.

Artichoke Pie

This quiche is the ultimate crowd-pleasing menu item that can be served warm or cold, really anytime, paired with salad, soup or fruit. I like to make this on a lazy Friday night since it goes a long way for the weekend.

SERVINGS: 8 slices | Prep Time: 10 minutes | Cooking Time: 60 minutes

INGREDIENTS:
1 9" deep dish pie crust - either homemade or store-bought (if frozen remove from freezer 15 minutes before filling)
1 - 14 ounce can of artichoke hearts - drain, chop and cut in half
2 cups of shredded whole milk mozzarella cheese
1/4 cup of shredded Parmigiano-Reggiano cheese
3 eggs
1 cup of ricotta cheese
1/2 teaspoon of salt
1 teaspoon of garlic powder
1/8 teaspoon of black pepper
1 tablespoon of fresh minced basil

DIRECTIONS:
1. Preheat oven to 350°F. In a large mixing bowl, beat the eggs together with the garlic powder, salt, black pepper, and the basil.

2. Add the artichokes shredded mozzarella and Parmigiano-Reggiano cheese as well as the ricotta cheese and mix well with a spatula and pour into the pie shell.

3. Bake at 350°F for an hour or until a toothpick inserted in the center comes out clean. This may be served hot or cold.

Mushroom Burrata Bruschetta with Lavender Balsamic

This earthy, creamy, and oh so dreamy, simple burr-ahhhh-ta appetizer will be your go-to for entertaining, even if it's just a party of one. Being a mushroom lover, for me, this was a no brainer, but this easily works just as well with tomatoes and basil or roasted peppers. If you've never had burrata cheese, it's a version of mozzarella that has a cream center - essentially a pocket of godliness. Being a bit milder and creamier than typical mozzarella, its oozy heavenly texture just begs to be spread on crispy bruschetta. This is the perfect way to salvage a loaf of Italian bread or baguette that is getting stale.

SERVINGS: 8-10 pieces | Prep Time: 10 minutes | Cooking Time: 10 minutes

INGREDIENTS:
2 cups of baby bella mushrooms, washed, dried and sliced
1 shallot, sliced
2 balls of burrata, at room temperature
1 garlic clove, minced
1 loaf of Italian bread or French baguette (seeded or unseeded, doesn't matter if it's 1-2 days old)
3 tablespoons of extra virgin olive oil, plus more for brushing
1-2 tablespoons of chopped parsley
3 tablespoons of lavender balsamic vinegar (you can also use more to boil it to reduce it and then cool it to make a thicker glaze)
Sea salt and pepper, to taste

DIRECTIONS:
1. Preheat oven to 425°F. In a large frying pan on medium heat, sauté the garlic and shallot in the olive oil, when soft add the mushroom and sauté until they are tender. Add salt and pepper to taste and set aside.

2. Prepare a baking sheet and line with parchment paper. Slice the bread diagonally approximately 1/2" to 3/4" slices. With a basting brush, brush each side of the bread slice with olive oil, sprinkle the parsley on the top of each. Sprinkle with salt and pepper to taste. Line up the bread in rows on the baking sheet and bake in the oven for 6-8 minutes, flipping mid-way until toasted and golden brown on both sides.

3. Pierce and spread the burrata generously on each of the bread slices. Top with the mushroom and shallot mixture. Drizzle with the lavender balsamic vinegar glaze and serve. This can also be served eliminating the bread just with the burrata and mushroom mixture as a cold salad, olive oil and lavender balsamic.

Classic Stromboli with Marinara Sauce

Who DOESN'T love this Italian-American pocket of goodness? Filled with all your favorite cured meats and cheeses, this rolled dough is sure a crowd-pleaser. Just roll it up, cut it up and enjoy! It's super easy and fun for the whole family to make and eat, whether it be for a Sunday dinner, a game day appetizer, or a snack!

Aside from being an island off the coast of Sicily, stromboli is actually an Italian-American creation of Nazzareno Romano "Nat" from South Philly in 1950 who named his restaurant's stuffed breads after a famous feature film of the same name at that time starring Ingrid Bergman and Roberto Rossellini. The best part about stromboli is you can customize it with whatever fillings you want, and even make it vegetarian with spinach, broccoli, or eggplant. This is the classic recipe which is overflowing with delicious ingredients just like the volcanic island itself. You definitely don't want to skip the side of marinara dipping sauce either - so simple to make and can totally be re-used to make a quick plate of amazing pasta. Buon Appetito!

SERVINGS: 8-10 pieces | Prep Time: 15 minutes | Cooking Time: 20-30 minutes

INGREDIENTS:

1 cup of shredded mozzarella
1 tablespoon of extra virgin olive oil
1/4 pound of Genoa salami slices
1/4 pound of pepperoni slices
1/4 pound of ham slices
3 tablespoons of grated Pecorino Romano cheese plus additional for sprinkling on top
1 pound of pizza dough (you can make your own or use refrigerated store or pizzeria bought)

1/4 pound of provolone cheese
1 egg, for brushing
1/4 cup of chopped parsley, for garnish
Sesame seeds, for garnish
1/4 pound of prosciutto

Marinara Sauce for dipping:
1 can crushed San Marzano tomatoes
2 cloves of garlic, chopped
4 basil leaves

1 teaspoon of salt
1 teaspoon of pepper
1/4 cup of extra virgin olive oil

* I find the cured meats supply enough seasoning, but some people add extra Italian or pizza seasoning to the inside. In my opinion, it takes away from the stromboli, but it's your preference.

DIRECTIONS:

1. Preheat oven to 400°F. Line a baking sheet with parchment paper.
2. Making sure you are working on a vast, smooth surface, roll out the room-temperature dough (sitting in a bowl covered with a cloth coated with a little olive oil) to a rectangle, to approximately 16" x 16."
3. Baste the surface of the dough with the olive oil on a brush.
4. Start by layering the cured meats and cheeses on the dough in rows - making sure to leave clearance of about 2 inches around each side. (Hint: Layer the ham and prosciutto vertically since you will be slicing the stromboli and it will make for a better bite). Sprinkle the mozzarella on top of the layers of meats and provolone. Top with the grated pecorino cheese.
5. Tightly roll the dough toward you like a jelly roll making sure to pat the end seam down and pinch both ends closed.
6. Place the roll, seam side down, on the baking sheet.
7. Baste the top and sides of the stromboli with the egg wash. Sprinkle some grated cheese on top, along with sesame seeds and chopped parsley.
8. Using a sharp knife, make several cute along the top of the stromboli for steam escape.
9. Bake for about 20-30 minutes or until golden brown. Check on it and turn it in the oven, as necessary, for even cooking. Allow it to cool 5 minutes. Slice the bread into about 8-10 pieces before serving with a side of the marinara sauce for dipping.

Marinara Sauce:
Prep Time: 5 minutes | Cooking Time: 15 minutes

1. Heat oil in a frying pan over low to medium heat. Add the garlic and sauté until golden brown, careful not to burn, approximately 3-4 minutes.

2. In a saucepan, over medium heat, add the can of crushed tomatoes, and transfer the garlic and oil into the saucepan. Add the salt and pepper. Cook approximately 10-12 minutes, stirring occasionally, adding basil toward the end of cooking.

Sausage Smoked Mozzarella Pumpkin and Sage Stromboli

The quintessential Italian-American food, I love a good stromboli and when the ingredients are seasonal, I'm all in. If you're looking for a unique autumn seasonal stromboli recipe, this one is for you. The sweetness of the pumpkin and sage are complemented by the smokiness of the mozzarella and the salty umami of the sausage creates layers on top of layers of flavor guaranteed to be as bit a hit in your home as it is in mine.

SERVINGS: 10-12 slices | Prep Time: 15 minutes | Cooking Time: 20-30 minutes

INGREDIENTS:
Pizza dough (you can make your own or use store-bought)
1 cup of pumpkin puree
1 1/2 cups of smoked mozzarella
4 tablespoons of grated Pecorino Romano cheese
3-4 chopped sage leaves
1 teaspoon of black pepper
1/2 teaspoon of salt
1 egg, for brushing
Sesame seeds, for outside
2 tablespoons of chopped parsley, for outside
4 Italian sausages out of the casing, browned with 1/4 cup of chopped onion.

Marinara Sauce for dipping:
1 can crushed San Marzano tomatoes
2 cloves of garlic, chopped
4 basil leaves
1 teaspoon of salt
1 teaspoon of pepper
1/4 cup of extra virgin olive oil

DIRECTIONS:
1. Preheat oven to 400°F. Roll out the dough and stretch it out over a piece of parchment paper over a baking cookie sheet. Spread the pumpkin puree leaving about 2 inches from the edge on all sides. Top with 3 of the tablespoons of grated cheese, shredded mozzarella, black pepper, sage and end with the browned sausage.

2. Roll up the dough like a cinnamon roll, careful to not push the ingredients out of the roll. Pinch the edges to seal and fold where the seam is. Lay the stromboli seam side down. Brush with the egg wash (which is the egg white plus 1 tablespoon of water) and cut approximately 8 small slats with the sharp knife across the top. Top with the parsley, 1 tablespoon of grated cheese and sprinkle with sesame seeds.

3. Bake for approximately 20-30 minutes or until golden brown on top. Serve with marinara sauce.

Marinara Sauce:
Prep Time: 5 minutes | Cooking Time: 15 minutes

1. Heat oil in a frying pan over low to medium heat. Add the garlic and sauté until golden brown, careful not to burn, approximately 3-4 minutes.

2. In a saucepan, over medium heat, add the can of crushed tomatoes, and transfer the garlic and oil into the saucepan. Add the salt and pepper. Cook approximately 10-12 minutes, stirring occasionally, adding basil toward the end of cooking.

Crab Cakes

Crabs have always been one of my favorite foods of all time. I don't know if it's their sweet and succulent taste or the fact that you have to work so hard at getting the meat, or maybe a little bit of both that makes them so alluring. There is just something about the ease of eating a pan-fried, seasoned crab cake that makes these even more special.

SERVINGS: 4 | Prep Time: 10 minutes | Cooking Time: 10 minutes

INGREDIENTS:
1 pound of jumbo lump crab meat
20 crushed Ritz® or saltine crackers
1 large beaten egg
1 tablespoon of Worcestershire sauce
1 tablespoon of Old Bay® seasoning
1 tablespoon of dijon mustard
1 teaspoon of hot sauce
1/2 cup of mayonnaise
1/2 cup of vegetable or canola oil
2 tablespoons of chopped parsley
Salt and black pepper, to taste
Lemon wedges and arugula bed, for serving

DIRECTIONS:
1. In a small bowl, combine the mayonnaise, egg, mustard, Worcestershire sauce, hot sauce, and Old Bay® seasoning, and parsley.

2. In a medium bowl, lightly toss the crabmeat and crackers and fold in the mayonnaise mixture. Cover and refrigerate for at least an hour.

3. Scoop the crab mixture and form into 8 small even patties about 1 1/2 inches thick or fewer larger ones (however you prefer). In a large deep skillet, heat the oil until shimmering. Add the crab cakes and cook over moderately high heat until deeply golden brown and heated through about 3 minutes on each side. Transfer the crab cakes to plates and serve with lemon wedges.

Spinach Bacon Quiche

All we are saying, is give quiche a chance. I love a good quiche recipe, and who doesn't love bacon? If you haven't tried it and aren't sold, it's like a cousin of an omelette or a frittata, but in a pie crust. So simple to make, it's like the gift that keeps giving. Perfect for a brunch or to bring to someone's house when they say, "just bring yourselves," this quiche is a huge hit.

SERVINGS: 8 Slices | Prep Time: 20 minutes | Cooking Time: 40 minutes

INGREDIENTS:
6 large eggs, beaten
1 1/2 cups of heavy cream
2 cups of chopped baby spinach - or 1-10 ounce package of frozen spinach, thawed, drained and squeezed dry.
3/4 pound of bacon - cooked, drained and cut up into bite-size pieces
1/2 cup of sautéed chopped onion
1/4 cup of grated Parmigiano Reggiano cheese
1 1/2 cups of shredded Swiss cheese
1 - 9" deep dish pie crust either homemade or store bought
Salt and pepper, to taste

DIRECTIONS:
1. Preheat the oven to 375°F.

2. Whisk or blend the eggs, cream, salt and pepper.

3. In a large mixing bowl, combine the spinach, sautéed onion, bacon, and cheese and mix well. Pour that mixture on top of the pie crust then pour the egg mixture on top. Bake for about 40 minutes until the egg mixture is set.

Thai Lettuce Wraps

Ready for a quick, easy and flavorful weeknight dinner? Or just an appetizer that is bursting with bold flavor and fresh ingredients? Say no more. These Thai Lettuce Wraps literally come together so effortlessly and are so light and healthy, perfect for warmer weather. Just 20 minutes, and that's a wrap!

SERVINGS: 4 | Prep Time: 10 minutes | Cooking Time: 10 minutes

INGREDIENTS:
1 tablespoon of extra virgin olive oil or vegetable oil
1 pound of ground chicken
2 cloves of garlic, minced
1 small white onion, diced
1/4 cup of hoisin sauce
2 tablespoons of soy sauce
1 tablespoon of rice wine vinegar
1 tablespoon of freshly grated ginger
1 tablespoon of Sriracha
1 can (8 ounces) of water chestnuts, drained and chopped
2 scallions thinly sliced, extra for garnish
Kosher salt and freshly ground black pepper, to taste
1 head of butter or romaine lettuce, whatever you prefer
1/2 cup of chopped peanuts

DIRECTIONS:
1. Add olive oil or vegetable oil and ground chicken to a large non-stick skillet. Cook and crumble over medium-high heat until browned, approximately 3-5 minutes. Drain any fat and excess water as it cooks.

2. Stir in garlic, onion, hoisin sauce, soy sauce, rice wine vinegar, ginger and Sriracha until onions have become translucent, about 2 minutes. Stir in water chestnuts and green onions until tender, about 1-2 minutes; season with salt and pepper to taste. Add chopped peanuts at the end and stir.

3. Spoon several tablespoons of the chicken mixture into the center of a lettuce leaf. Serve immediately and enjoy!

Mom's Simple Classic Chili

Being Italian-American, I have the luxury of having Italian comfort food favorites and American comfort food favorites and growing up, a bowl of my mom's chili was definitely one of my favorite American traditional comfort foods with a "kick" that I still treasure. It's no wonder that come fall and winter, thousands of Americans make it every day for parties, tailgates or just for a quiet lunch or dinner at home. This is so good that you won't be able to stop going back for spoonfuls. Not only is this classic chili recipe amazingly flavorful and easy, you can use it as a template to make it your own - whether it be vegetarian, chicken, turkey, chorizo or with other spices and toppings.

SERVINGS: 12 | Prep Time: 35 minutes | Cooking Time: 90 minutes

INGREDIENTS:

1 Anaheim chili pepper, chopped
2 red jalapeño peppers chopped
1-2 green jalapeño peppers for garnish
4 minced garlic cloves
2 1/2 pounds of lean ground beef*
2 - 16-ounce cans of kidney beans
1 pinch of garlic powder, to taste
2 cubes of beef bouillon
1 can of fire-roasted diced tomatoes
1 - 28 ounce can of San Marzano Tomatoes
2 tablespoons of chili powder

1 tablespoons of ground cumin
1 large yellow onion, diced
1 tablespoon of chipotle pepper sauce
1/4 cup of Worcestershire sauce
3 tablespoons of extra virgin olive oil
1 small can of tomato paste
1 teaspoon of brown sugar
1 1/2 teaspoons of smoked paprika
1 teaspoon of salt
1 teaspoon of black pepper

2 cups of shredded cheddar, 1 cup of sour cream, 1 cup of diced red onion are optional to garnish.
Serve on top of your favorite rice - optional

*you can substitute ground turkey or Beyond Beef® as an alternative in the same quantity and same preparation.

DIRECTIONS:

1. Over a medium heat, heat the oil in a large pot and stir in the onion, jalapeños, Anaheim pepper and garlic until onion is translucent and everything is softened.

2. In a separate large skillet over medium to high flame, stir in the beef until browned and crumbly, breaking up the pieces with a wooden spoon, about 6-8 minutes. Add the Worcestershire sauce and garlic powder and crumbled bouillon cubes. Mix well and continue to sauté, scraping the skillet for any brown bits about 3-4 minutes. Combine the beef mixture with the onion/pepper mixture into the large pot.

3. Mix in the crushed San Marzano tomatoes, diced tomatoes and the tomato paste, as well as wine. Add the chili powder, cumin, brown sugar, paprika, salt and pepper. Bring the mixture to a boil then lower the flame to a simmer. Cover it and cook until the vegetables are tender, and the flavors have all incorporated into the chili, about 60 minutes. Stirring occasionally.

4. Mix the kidney beans into the chili. Simmer for about 20-30 minutes more, adding water to dilute to prefered thickness.

5. Serve with melted shredded cheddar cheese, a dollop of sour cream, red onions, and extra sliced jalapeños on top of each portion if desired.

Buffalo Chicken Dip

This dip is a sinfully creamy and tangy mouthwatering appetizer infused with hot wing flavors, but without the mess. Whenever I bring this dip to a Super Bowl party or tailgate everyone asks for my recipe. Best served warm, with crackers, celery and carrots, it's a total winner.

SERVINGS: 4 | Prep Time: 20 minutes | Cooking Time: 20 minutes

INGREDIENTS:
1 - 8-ounce package of room temperature cream cheese
2 large chicken breasts*
2 bouillon cubes
3/4 cup of Frank's Red Hot® Buffalo (or mild) Wing Sauce
1/2 cup of shredded cheddar cheese
1/2 cup of bleu cheese dressing
1/2 cup of bleu cheese crumbles
3 chopped scallions
Cut up celery and carrots
Crackers or chips for dipping

DIRECTIONS:
1. Preheat oven to 350°F.

2. Rinse and boil chicken in a medium stockpot with bouillon until fully cooked (white inside, not pink). Remove and allow it to cool. Shred chicken in a large mixing bowl. Mix in all the other ingredients except for the scallions and crumbled blue cheese.

3. Spoon into a medium 12" cast iron pan or shallow 1-quart baking dish.

4. Bake for 20 minutes until mixture is heated through. Stir. Sprinkle the scallions and crumbled blue cheese on top. Serve with cut-up veggies and/or crackers and chips.

*you could also use store-cooked rotisserie chicken shredded up if pressed for time.

Italian Friselle Wreaths

Like many Italian-American families, we could never have enough festive recipes for the holidays. Friselle are a toasted bread, typical of the southernmost part of Puglia in Italy and often served with bruschetta. Friselle wreath adorned with sautéed broccoli rabe, olives, hot peppers and sundried tomato bows are always a big hit on the Christmas table when the antipasto comes out.

✕

SERVINGS: 6 - 8 | Prep Time: 20 minutes | Cooking Time: 1 hour

INGREDIENTS:
2 cups of all-purpose flour
1 cup of whole wheat flour
1 1/4 cup of lukewarm water
1 teaspoon of active dry yeast
1 teaspoon of salt
2 teaspoons of freshly ground black pepper
2 tablespoons of extra virgin olive oil

DIRECTIONS:
1. Preheat over to 480°F.

2. Mix yeast in lukewarm water and let sit for 10 minutes, stirring well until the yeast is dissolved.

3. In the bowl of a stand mixer, add the flour as well as the yeast-water mix. Knead on low with the dough hook attachment, slowly increasing the speed to high. You can also do this by hand.

4. Add a pinch of salt, pepper, and the olive oil. Knead for another 1-2 minutes until the dough is smooth but still soft and has a slightly sticky consistency.

5. Transfer to a large bowl coated with olive oil. Cover with plastic wrap and let sit for approximately 2 hours in a warm place until it is just about doubled in bulk.

6. Generously flour a work surface or a large donut mold pan. Turn the bowl of dough upside down. Divide it into 6-8 equal parts, depending on how large or small you desire the friselle to be.

7. Use your hands to roll each piece against the work surface to approximately 6 inches in length. Lightly pat it and make a hole with your finger or the end of a wooden spoon through the center and fold each dough log forming a circle like a bagel shape, securing the ends. Or, if you are using a donut mold, you can mold the dough into the greased molds, leaving generous space for them to rise.

8. If molding yourself, place the friselle on a baking pan lined with parchment paper and let rise for 40-60 minutes until they double in size.

9. Bake at 480°F for about 12-15 minutes. Allow them to cool on a wire rack until you can safely touch the friselle without burning your hands.

10. Cut each of the friselle in half using a sharp serrated bread knife and return them to the baking sheet cut side up. Bake for 30-40 minutes at 350°F. Allow them to cool on a wire rack.

Top with sauteéd broccoli rabe (in garlic and oil), green and black olives, marinated sundried tomatoes and hot pepper rings.

Soups

One-Pot Sausage Ribollita

Toscano (Tuscany) in Italy is a very special place to me - I have been fortunate enough to have traveled to this beautiful sunflower-adorned region several times and in my travels this was one dish that stole my heart (and my appetite).

Ribollita is a famous, centuries-old hearty Tuscan bread soup made with bread and vegetables. There are many variations but the main ingredients always include leftover bread, cannellini beans, lacinato kale and inexpensive vegetables such as carrots, beans, chard, celery potatoes, onion and garlic. This soup often features crispy bacon for a hint of smoky, meaty richness, but I find making it with crumbled sausage adds a delicious complex flavor and texture profile that is unmatched.

Although the flavors of this soup are complex, it is deceptively easy to make. Who doesn't love a one-pot meal? "Ribollita" is a bit of a misnomer. It translates to "reboiled," but that just means that it is a leftover soup thickened with day-old bread. This kind of dish is typical to la cucina povera, a traditional style of Italian cuisine that literally translates to "poor cooking." Maybe poor cooking, but undoubtedly rich in flavor.

SERVINGS: 4 | Prep Time: 20 minutes | Cooking Time: 40 minutes

INGREDIENTS:

6 Italian sausages, out of the casing
3 tablespoons of extra virgin olive oil
1 small onion, chopped
1 shallot, chopped
1 large carrot, diced
3 sprigs of rosemary, chopped
4-6 cups of low sodium chicken stock
Salt and pepper, to taste
5 large slices of old crusty sourdough, peasant or Italian panella bread + more for dipping

1 large bunch of lacinato kale (black kale), leaves cut into 2" pieces
1 tablespoon of dry cooking wine
1 19 ounce can of Cannellini beans
2 celery sticks, diced
3 large finely chopped garlic cloves
1 can or box of diced tomatoes (approximately 14 ounce)
3/4 teaspoon of red pepper flakes
Parmigiano-Reggiano rind + more grated for serving

DIRECTIONS:

1. Heat a large deep nonstick oven safe pot and add the sausage meat which was removed from the casings. Break up with a wooden spoon and brown for about 5-6 minutes until fully cooked. Remove to a plate.

2. Add the oil to the pan, then the onion, shallot, celery and carrot, and cook gently, covered on low heat, for approximately 10 minutes, stirring occasionally. Stir in the rosemary and garlic. Cook for about 2 minutes. Add the tomatoes. chicken stock, wine, cheese rind and red pepper flakes. Bring to a boil and simmer for 10 minutes.

3. Add the drained cannellini beans and sausage. Simmer for 10 minutes. Add the kale, cover and cook for 3-4 minutes.

4. Ladle the stew into bowls, drizzle generously with olive oil and grated cheese over each potion. Serve with extra cheese and crusty bread, salt and pepper to taste.

Some people take the finished soup and remove it from the heat and place half the amount of bread, broken into pieces in the soup, stirring occasionally and warmed through about 5 minutes and add the remainder of the bread chunks on top of the soup, drizzling with olive oil and bake it in the oven at 400°F approximately 10-15 minutes or until the bread on top is golden brown. A classic ribollita is cooked one day, then reheated and served the next. To do that, just refrain from putting the last pieces of bread so they stay crunchy.

Pasta and Peas - red style (Pasta e Piselli)

This simple, delicious one-pot wonder is just how my Napoletana Nana made it. Ideal with a short pasta like elbows, shells or ditalini (I always like making it with shells - when I was young, I used to like how the peas hid in the shells like pearls in an oyster). It's on the table in under 30 minutes. The perfect dish to make to impress your date who, at first bite, will mistakenly believe you toiled in the kitchen for hours. It's so economical, quick and so tasty you will find yourself making it over and over again.

SERVINGS: 4-6 | Prep Time: 10 minutes | Cooking Time: 20 minutes

INGREDIENTS:
1 pound of short pasta (shells, elbows, ditalini, etc.)
1 large yellow onion, diced
2 - 28-ounce cans of crushed San Marzano Tomatoes
Extra virgin olive oil to coat the bottom of the pan
2 cups or 16 ounces of frozen peas
Salt and pepper, to taste
Freshly grated Pecorino Romano cheese, to taste
Pepperoncino (crushed red pepper), to taste

DIRECTIONS:
1. Over low to medium heat, coat the bottom of a large deep sauté pan with olive oil and when hot, sauté the large diced onion until translucent, careful not to burn, about 5-7 minutes.

2. Add the tomatoes to the oil-onion mixture, add salt and pepper to taste, and heat on medium for about 15 minutes, stirring occasionally.

3. Put up a medium size pot of salted boiling water and cook pasta according to package directions until al dente.

4. Add the 2 cups of frozen peas to the tomato sauce and mix about 5 more minutes (I also add freshly grated cheese to taste during this step).

5. Drain the pasta, reserving 1 cup of pasta water to mix in. Add the cooked pasta to the tomatoes, peas, and reserved pasta water. Give it a stir and sprinkle grated cheese and red pepper, and serve with Italian bread if desired. Enjoy!

French Onion Soup

This soup doesn't need much of an introduction. Arguably the king of soups, and one of my absolute favorites, we can't have a conversation about soups unless you include French Onion. This wasn't a soup that we had at home growing up, rather it was always one I would order in a restaurant and feel like a little socialite eating. As I got older, I explored different recipes, and this would be one that goes in the self-taught category. There is so much flavor in this soup between the richest caramelized onion flavors, copious amounts of melted Gruyère cheese and topped with a crunchy baguette crouton, it is a soup that is guaranteed to be a hit with the whole family, down to the pickiest eaters. Perfect with a chilled white wine such as a Sancerre, you have yourself a perfect satisfying meal, without traveling to Paris.

SERVINGS: 8 | Prep Time: 35 minutes | Cooking Time: 35 minutes

INGREDIENTS:
8 cups of yellow onions, thinly sliced
1/2 cup of unsalted butter
1 bay leaf
2 thyme sprigs
8 cups of beef stock or mushroom stock
1/4 cup of sherry or Marsala
1 cup of dry white wine
1 baguette
Salt and pepper, to taste
1/2 pound of grated Gruyère cheese (I prefer it aged) and 1 pound of muenster cheese
Parsley, to garnish

DIRECTIONS:
1. Place a medium stockpot, on medium-high heat, add butter, onions, type and the bay leaf and sauté until the onions turn golden brown and caramelized (this can take up to 25-30 minutes). Deglaze the pan with the sherry or Marsala and cook for 2 minutes. Add the white wine and cook uncovered for about 15 minutes. Add the stock and season with salt and pepper to taste. Bring to a boil, then cook uncovered for 20 minutes. Ladle the soup into broiler-safe bowls or crocks.

2. Cut the baguette into 16 slices cut on a bias, sizing them so that 2 slices fit inside each bowl or crock. Arrange the bread slices on a baking broil, turning once, until lightly toasted on both sides, about 1-2 minutes total. Set the slices aside. Position the oven rack about 12 inches from the heat source and leave the broiler on.

3. Place 2 toasted bread slices, overlapping if necessary, on top of the soup and sprinkle each crock evenly with the Gruyère and muenster, and parsley. Broil until the cheese is bubbling, about 2-3 minutes. Serve at once.

Chicken Soup

The ultimate comfort food, chicken soup is just as much for the soul and mind as it is the belly. Whether you use ditalini, tubettini, acini di pepe, pastina or rice in it, everyone undoubtedly has a different chicken soup recipe. I learned mine from my beloved Nana Angie. For me, with the slightest Fall breeze or cold rain, the stock pots come right out. Curing all ills from the second it begins to boil, the aroma alone permeating the house is better than any plug-in or air freshener I know. And the best part is all the leftovers, which can be frozen for those rushed weekday lunches or dinners when you have no time to cook.

SERVINGS: 12 | Prep Time: 20 minutes | Cooking Time: 2 hours

INGREDIENTS:
1 3-pound whole chicken
1 pound of short pasta
2 48-ounce boxes of chicken broth (or bouillon cubes with water)
2 parsnips, chopped
2 turnips, chopped
5 carrots, chopped
5 celery stalks, chopped
2 onions, one chopped, one whole
2 tablespoons of fresh parsley, chopped
2 tablespoons of fresh dill, chopped
Salt and pepper

DIRECTIONS:
1. Rinse the chicken under cold water and remove the gizzards/neck packet if it is enclosed and discard (some use this, I don't – it's your preference). Peel an onion and stick it inside in the chicken whole. Simmer uncovered in a large stockpot with 1 box of broth and additional water so it is submerged. Add 1 tablespoon of salt and 1 teaspoon of pepper.

2. Let the chicken simmer for about an hour and a half skimming foam off the top occasionally while it boils. Then add onion, parsley, turnip, parsnip, dill (whatever you like) let it simmer and keep skimming foam. Add more stock, and any additional salt and pepper to taste. When the flesh is tender enough to shred without effort, remove the chicken and shred it. I use all the chicken for the soup but you can use some and save some for other uses. I boil my celery and carrots separately over the stove because I like them on the firmer side and throw them in the soup at the end.

3. You can make it even healthier and the broth even clearer by refrigerating the broth so the fat hardens and accumulates on the surface, then scoop it off.

4. Bring a separate pot of salted water to a boil for the pasta, rice or noodles. Once cooked, combine with the chicken soup, celery and carrots.

Pasta and Peas with Bacon (Pasta e Piselli)

Every cook has a signature dish and this would definitely be my mom's. Everyone, including my family, loves when she makes Pasta e Piselli to this day. She taught me how to make it years ago when my son Luca was 2 years old, as he would gobble it up in his high chair. Since there's wine and Marsala in it he and my nieces would eat so much of it, we were concerned that perhaps they would sleep a little too well after dinner but the doctor said not to worry as it all burns off in cooking! A simple, delicious and affordable meal that will certainly become a family staple. Make sure to top it with lots of cheese!

SERVINGS: 6 | Prep Time: 10 minutes | Cooking Time: 20 minutes

INGREDIENTS:
1 pound of short pasta (shells, elbows, ditalini etc.)
1 large diced white onion
1 minced large garlic clove
3 cups of frozen peas
1/4 cup of extra virgin olive oil
2 cups of chicken stock
1/2 cup of cooking sherry
1/2 cup of Marsala cooking wine
1 pound of bacon, cut into 1" squares
Salt and pepper, to taste
Grated Parmigiano-Reggiaro cheese, for serving

DIRECTIONS:
1. On a medium heat in a large saucepan, sauté the onions and garlic in olive oil until translucent.

2. Separately, in a skillet, sauté the bacon until fully cooked but not burned. Combine the contents of the bacon skillet, fat and all, into the onion and garlic mixture. Add chicken stock, sherry and Marsala to your saucepan and simmer on low for 5-7 minutes. Add salt and pepper.

3. In a separate pasta pot, boil your salted water for the pasta. While pasta is boiling, add peas to sauce pot containing the broth mixture. Take pasta out al dente, reserving 1 cup of salted pasta water. Combine pasta into the broth, peas, wine and bacon mixture. Stir on a very low simmer, adding the pasta water to dilute to desired consistency. Grate cheese when serving, if desired.

If you prefer, you can prepare the peas and bacon sauce in advance, refrigerate it, and boil the pasta on the day you are making it. Leftovers also taste great reheated. I reheat mine in a cast-iron skillet with a teaspoon of olive oil.

Pumpkin Apple Bisque

Fall being my second favorite season, I'm a sucker for anything pumpkin. Crisp leaves, cool temperatures, and apple picking always inspire me to make this hearty and healthy soup. Even without the added cream, this bisque takes on a luxuriously velvety texture after its simmered and puréed. Naturally gluten-free, vegan, and, if you eliminate the cream, dairy free, this soup to table in under an hour.

SERVINGS: 6 | Prep Time: 10 minutes | Cooking Time: 70 minutes

INGREDIENTS:
3 pounds of sugar pumpkin, seeded and halved or you can use canned purée instead
3 tablespoons of butter
1 shallot, finely chopped
3 Granny Smith apples, diced
1 minced garlic clove
1 teaspoon of light brown sugar
1 tablespoon of red apple balsamic (I used one from Saratoga Olive Oil Co.)
1/4 teaspoon of white pepper
1/4 teaspoon of cayenne pepper
1/4 teaspoon of ground nutmeg
1/2 teaspoon of ground cinnamon
3 cups of low sodium vegetable broth
1 teaspoon of apple cider vinegar
Sea salt
1/2 cup of heavy whipping cream
1/2 Granny Smith apple diced for garnish
Pepitas (pumpkin seeds) for garnish

DIRECTIONS:
1. Preheat oven to 400°F. Brush the pumpkin and apple with vegetable or grapeseed oil and sprinkle with salt. Place them face-down on a baking sheet in the oven for 30 minutes or until fork-tender. Remove from oven and when cooled, scoop out the pumpkin. Set those aside.

2. In a large pot over a medium flame, melt the butter and sauté the shallot for about 3-5 minutes. Add the diced apple, brown sugar, garlic, white pepper, cayenne, nutmeg and cinnamon, along with the broth, while stirring. Reduce to simmer for 20 minutes, then fold in the cream and let cool for about 15 minutes.

3. Transfer everything to a blender (or use a hand-held immersion blender) to smooth out the consistency. If you prefer a thinner soup, just add a little water or more broth to reach your desired consistency. Return to a saucepan and reheat for a couple of minutes, then garnish with apples, pepitas and a dollop of cream.

Main Courses

Linguine Puttanesca

Sometimes in life, you just have to work with what you have. Keep it simple. Enter Linguine Puttanesca. Lidia Bastianich once said, "Italian food is seasonal. It is simple. It is nutritionally sound. It is flavorful. It is colorful. It's all the things that make for a good eating experience, and it's good for you." The same attributes could be said about Linguine Puttanesca made with pantry staples we already have in our homes.

The origins of this Napoletana dish from the mid-20th century are rather intriguing. There are many explanations for the origin of puttanesca, and almost as many ways to make it. Rumored to be a sauce invented by prostitutes (some say the name originated in the brothels of the Spanish Quarters - whore is "puttana" in Italian, hence puttanesca). Some scholars have tried to trace the first inventive chef who began to call this spicy dish 'puttanesca.' Originally called "alla marinara," this current name began to appear after World War II. Others claimed it was invented in the 1950's in a famous restaurant in Ischia one late night when a group of hungry customers asked the owner, who did not have many ingredients left, to make "una puttana qualsiasi," that is, to throw together whatever ingredients he had to make something simple. The owner only had some tomatoes, olives and capers, the base for the sauce, and that's how he came up with the puttanesca sauce. Some indeed say the modern name of this preparation refers to pasta "prepared as it comes," that is, easy to cook without frills or complicated preparation. Puttanesca can be made with or without anchovies and is so easy to make and teach to beginning chefs.

SERVINGS: 4 | Prep Time: 5 minutes | Cooking Time: 20 minutes

INGREDIENTS:
1 pound of linguine or other long pasta
3 tablespoons of extra virgin olive oil
3 chopped garlic cloves
4 anchovy filets in oil
1 28 ounce can of whole peeled San Marzano tomatoes
1 cup of oil-cured black olives
3 tablespoons of rinsed capers
Freshly ground black pepper
Crushed red pepper flakes, to taste
Chopped fresh parsley and or basil, for garnish

DIRECTIONS:
1. In a large bowl, drain the tomatoes and crush them with hands or crusher and set aside.

2. Heat 2 tablespoons of olive oil on a skillet and brown the garlic and anchovies over low to medium heat.

3. Add the tomatoes to the skillet with some salt and pepper. Raise the flame to medium and let it sauté, while stirring, for about 10 minutes. Then stir in the olives, capers and red pepper flakes. Lower it to simmer.

4. Cook the pasta al dente in salted water. Drain it and toss the linguine in the skillet with one tablespoon of olive oil. Taste it and add salt if needed (it is already salted due to the capers and anchovies so you may not need any). Garnish with parsley and/or basil.

Lamb Burgers with Feta Tzatziki Sauce

Don't get me wrong, l love a good ole fashioned cheesy all-American beef burger, but one bite of these Mediterranean lamb patties, loaded with all sorts of spices and herbs and slathered with homemade creamy cucumber Tzakiki sauce, and everything will be all Greek to you. And if you want to turn this simple meal into an epic Mediterranean picnic, you can make some delicious sauteed okra, a Greek salad or some Greek fries to go along with it.

SERVINGS: 4-8 depending on the thickness of the burgers | Prep Time: 20 minutes | Cooking Time: 10 minutes

INGREDIENTS:

2 pounds of ground lamb
2 small red onion, 1 minced and one sliced for serving
2 cloves of garlic, minced
1 egg
1 cup of fresh chopped parsley
1/2 cup of chopped mint leaves
2 teaspoons of ground cumin
1 teaspoon of coriander
1/2 teaspoon of paprika
1 teaspoon of oregano
Pinch of crushed red pepper (optional)

1/2 teaspoon of cayenne (optional)
Zest of 1/2 lemon
2 teaspoons of Kosher salt
1 teaspoon of black pepper
1 beefsteak tomato, for serving
Extra virgin olive oil
4 whole wheat pitas or 4 Portuguese buns
2 cups of baby spinach, for serving
Homemade Tzatziki sauce (see below)
Pitted Kalamata olives, for serving
Sliced feta, for serving

DIRECTIONS:

1. Prepare the meat mixture by adding the ground lamb to a mixing bowl. Add the egg, onions, garlic, herbs, coriander, oregano, cumin, paprika, red pepper, cayenne, parsley, mint, and lemon zest. Season with kosher salt and pepper. Add a generous drizzle of olive oil and mix together thoroughly.

2. Divide the meat mixture into anywhere from 4 to 8 equal balls. Using your hands, lightly press the meat to form patties. Arrange the patties on a baking tray lined with parchment paper. Cover and refrigerate until ready to cook on an outdoor grill or cast-iron skillet.

3. Lightly oil the grill grates or skillet with olive oil or butter and arrange the burgers on top. Grill over medium heat, covered for 4-5 minutes on each side, until browned, flipping midway (internal temperature for lamb should be 145°F). Adjust cooking time according to your desired doneness.

4. Allow the burgers to rest for about 5 minutes before serving. Serve in pita or buns with Tzatziki sauce, sliced beefsteak tomato, spinach and a slice of feta.

Feta Tzatziki Sauce

INGREDIENTS:

2 cups of plain Greek yogurt
1/2 cup of crumbled feta
1 tablespoon of white vinegar
2 cloves of minced garlic

2 sprigs of mint
1 small bunch of dill, finely chopped
1/2 seedless cucumber, coarsely grated
Kosher salt and pepper, to taste

DIRECTIONS:

Combine all ingredients. Season with salt and pepper to taste. Allow to sit about an hour at room temperature before serving on burgers.

Trofie with Pesto alla Genovese

A cornerstone of Ligurian cuisine, Trofie al pesto Genovese is a prime example that, with most Italian cooking, simplicity at the table always wins. The best pesto I ever had was in Santa Margarita Ligure, in Northwest Italy, about 35 kilometers south of Genoa. In my opinion, having pesto without using a Trofie cut of pasta is like having a martini in a rocks glass. You can do it, but why wouldn't you want it in its ideal form? It would be delicious, but why not have this ideal cut of pasta originating in its birthplace. It is believed that the women there would sit together in chairs along the coast and twist the pasta dough while waiting for their husbands to return from fishing excursions. Pesto is such a simple and uncooked recipe using 7 ingredients. It is ideal for a weeknight pasta meal, makes a delicious base sauce for a pizza, a spread on sandwiches, and even as an addition to savory waffles.

SERVINGS: 4 | Prep Time: 15 minutes | Cooking Time: None for the sauce, just for the pasta according to package directions

The authentic Italian way to make pesto (which is derived from the verb "pestare," to pound or grind) is with a mortar and pestle. This allows for a richer texture and definition among the ingredients. However, many modern day people use a blender or food processor to combine the ingredients for convenience. This method still produces a tasty pesto but the texture is a more uniform paste or homogeneous emulsion which lacks the depth of the original way. I prefer the authentic way. Both ways of making it appear below.

INGREDIENTS:
1 pound of trofie (or trenette) pasta
1/2 teaspoon of Kosher salt
2 cups of rinsed and dried fresh basil leaves, packed - the small leaves are the most flavorful
1/4 cup of freshly grated Parmigiano-Reggiano cheese, extra if desired for serving
1/4 cup of freshly grated Pecorino Sardo or Pecorino Romano cheese, extra if desired for serving.
3 garlic cloves, minced
1/3 cup of pignoli nuts, extra for garnish
1/2 cup of extra virgin olive oil

DIRECTIONS:

Mortar & Pestle Method:
1. In a large mortar, add the pignoli nuts, salt, and garlic cloves. Using a large pestle, pound and scrape the ingredients into a very smooth paste, 5–7 minutes. Add the basil in small amounts, working it into the mixture after each addition, until all the basil has been added and the mixture is smooth and creamy, 15–20 minutes.

2. Slowly add the oil while stirring with the pestle until emulsified. Add both cheeses and stir with the pestle to incorporate.

Food Processor Method:
1. In a food processor or blender, pulse the basil and pine nuts until finely chopped.

2. Add the garlic and both cheeses, and continue pulsing, stopping a couple of times to scrape the sides of the blender or food processor canister with a rubber spatula for the remnants.

3. While the food processor or blender is running, stream in the olive oil gingerly in a small stream. This will help it emulsify and prevent the oil from separating. Stop blending a few times to continue scraping the remnants from the sides with the spatula.

4. Stir in the salt and pepper, add more to taste.

5. Bring a salted pot of water to rapid boil and cook the pasta al dente according to package directions, about 8-10 minutes, retaining 1 cup of reserved pasta water. Toss the pesto with the steaming, strained pasta. Add 1 additional tablespoon of olive oil for more even coating of the sauce and pasta water to desired consistency.

Italian Sheet Pan Chicken

Time and time again, the Mediterranean diet has been deemed the healthiest way to eat, but the word diet connotes flavorless and that couldn't be further from the truth. I love an easy and healthy all in one sheet pan recipe, especially on a weeknight. Way too delicious to be relegated to a second course, this will be a tried and true family favorite. A word to the wise - you'll want to reserve some of the delicious tangy marinade to drizzle on the crusty Italian bread croutons.

SERVINGS: 4 | Prep Time: 20 minutes | Cooking Time: 55 minutes

INGREDIENTS:
1 whole chicken, large cut up with breasts quartered, skin on
1/2 cup of balsamic vinegar
2 teaspoons of dried parsley flakes
2 teaspoons of dried basil
1 teaspoon of kosher salt
1/2 teaspoon of freshly cracked black pepper
5 garlic cloves, minced
1 fresh lemon
1 cup plus 3 tablespoons of extra virgin olive oil
1 pound or more of green beans, rinsed and ends trimmed
2 cups of mixed heirloom tomatoes
1 loaf crusty seeded Italian bread
2 tablespoons of minced fresh parsley

DIRECTIONS:
1.Preheat oven to 425°F.

2. In a small mixing bowl, add the vinegar, parsley, basil, lemon, salt, pepper, garlic and 1 cup of the olive oil. Whisk until well combined.

3. Put the chicken in a large zipper bag and pour in half the dressing. Seal the bag and squish around completely coating the chicken.

4. Slice the tomatoes in half and put them and the string beans in a large mixing bowl. Pour the remaining dressing over the green beans and tomatoes and toss.

5. Using tongs, arrange the chicken, skin-side up, on a sheet pan. Use a slotted spoon to transfer the green beans and tomatoes to the sheet pan, leaving the excess marinade behind. Roast for about 45 minutes, shaking the pan midway to prevent sticking (if you like the green beans on the firmer side like I do, cook the chicken for 30 minutes then add the green beans and tomatoes for the last 10-15 minutes.)

6. Meanwhile, rip the bread into large chunks. Add to a bowl, drizzle with the remaining 3 tablespoons olive oil, some salt, pepper and dried basil and parsley and toss.

7. Add the bread chunks to the pan. Continue to roast until chicken is cooked through and the skin is golden and crisp, about another 10 minutes. Sprinkle the sheet pan with fresh parsley and serve.

Spicy Shrimp with Cheesy Creamy Polenta

Cajun Italian Fusion cuisine at its best. Polenta, for those of you who are not familiar, is typically a northern Italian dish made of coarsely ground corn. Freshly cooked, polenta is soft and creamy, like porridge or mush, and it makes a terrific bed for sauces. Once considered a humble peasant food, polenta has had a renaissance. It is now considered a fine-dining Italian comfort food and can be prepared in many different and delicious ways, including baked, fried and grilled, both creamy and firm. The combination of the smoked paprika, cajun spice and green chili flavors coating the shrimp with the sharpness of the cheddar and the buttery, cheesy cornmeal, is a marriage made in heaven, without having to book a flight anywhere.

SERVINGS: 4 | Prep Time: 10 minutes | Cooking Time: 30 minutes

INGREDIENTS: Polenta
2 cups of 2% or whole milk
2 cups of water
1 cup of course grain polenta
5 tablespoons of salted butter
3/4 cup of shredded cheddar cheese
Kosher salt and black pepper, to taste

INGREDIENTS: Shrimp
1 pound of large deveined and cleaned shrimp
1/4 cup of extra virgin olive oil
1 teaspoon of smoked paprika
1/4 teaspoon of kosher salt
1/4 teaspoon of black pepper
1/4 teaspoon of cayenne pepper
1 teaspoon of Cajun seasoning
1 teaspoon of ground cumin
1/2 teaspoon of adobo

INGREDIENTS: Sauce
1 14.5 ounce can of diced tomatoes
2 green chili peppers
2 cloves of minced garlic
1 teaspoon of extra virgin olive oil
1 teaspoon of smoked paprika
Kosher salt and black pepper, to taste

DIRECTIONS:
For Polenta:
1. In a large deep skillet, add water and milk. Bring to a boil and slowly whisk in the polenta. Once all the polenta has been added lower the heat to simmer and slowly whisk until thick. This usually takes about 5 to 7 minutes. Once it is creamy and cooked, remove it from the heat and stir in the butter, cheese, salt and pepper.

For Shrimp:
2. In a medium size mixing bowl, combine shrimp, olive oil, Cajun seasoning, smoked paprika, kosher salt, pepper, cayenne pepper, cumin, and adobo. Toss together until all the shrimp are completely coated.

3. In a large skillet over medium to high heat add the shrimp and cook until they are pink. Remove from the heat. Place the shrimp on a plate and wipe out the skillet. Be careful not to overcook or they will become rubbery.

For the Sauce:
4. You can use the same wiped skillet in which you cooked the shrimp, or you can use a small saucepan. Add the diced tomatoes, oil, smoked paprika, garlic and kosher salt and pepper to taste. Cool on medium until the mixture is hot. Add the shrimp to the tomatoes and serve on top of the polenta bed.

Caramelized Shallot Pasta with Toasted Bread Crumbs

Shallot we? We shall. I first made this recipe on a Sunday, since for me, right off the bat that meant pasta, but I wanted to change it up and had this recipe from New York Times Cooking earmarked as it was one of the recipes with Best of 2020 status. Only I amped it up a bit once I saw that anchovies were involved - enter the toasted garlicky breadcrumbs. I love anything with shallots, to me they're like onions without the chutzpah, sweet and flavorful with ladylike grace, but still tough enough to make you cry. Shallots very much take center stage here. This dish is definitely off the beaten path and if you're looking for a unique pasta recipe with a wow factor, this is it. It has a bit of a kick, but can always be made mild. And the leftover jammy-esque sauce can be used for so many other things - with eggs or spread on bruschetta.

SERVINGS: 4 | Prep Time: 10 minutes | Cooking Time: 40 minutes

INGREDIENTS:
1/4 cup plus 2 tablespoons of extra virgin olive oil
6 large shallots, very thinly sliced
5 garlic cloves, 4 thinly sliced and 2 finely chopped
Kosher salt and freshly ground black pepper
1 teaspoon of crushed red pepper flakes plus more for serving
1 - 2 ounce can of anchovy fillets, about 12, drained
1 4.5-ounce tube of tomato paste or about 1/2 to 3/4 cup
1 pound of long pasta, preferably bucatini, linguine or spaghetti
1 cup of finely chopped parsley
1 1/2 cups of fresh bread crumbs, toasted
Flaky sea salt

DIRECTIONS:
1. Heat olive oil in a large heavy-bottomed pan or Dutch oven over medium high heat. Add shallots and thinly sliced garlic, and season with salt and pepper. Cook and stir occasionally until the shallots have become caramelized with golden-brown fried edges, about 15-20 minutes.

2. Add crushed red pepper and anchovies. You could add the anchovies whole, since they will dissolve on their own. Stir to melt the anchovies to make a mixture with the shallots, about 2 minutes.

3. Add the tomato paste and season with salt and pepper. Cook, stirring constantly to prevent any burning until the tomato paste has started to cook in the oil, caramelizing at the edges and going from bright red to a deeper brick red color, about 2 minutes. Remove from the heat. To serve, cook the pasta in a large pot of salted boiling water according to package directions until very al dente. Transfer to the original pan or Dutch oven containing the shallot mixture. Add one cup of retained pasta water. Cook over medium high heat, swirling the pan to coat each strand of pasta, using a wooden spoon or spatula to scrape up any bits on the bottom, until pasta is thick, and the sauce has reduced to a sticky consistency, but not saucy, about 3-5 minutes.

4. In a large nonstick skillet, heat 2 tablespoons of olive oil and sauteé the breadcrumbs over low-medium heat, adding the parsley and finely chopped garlic clove, and flaky sea salt and pepper until bronzed.

5. In a small bowl, combine the parsley and finely chopped garlic clove, season with flaky salt and pepper. Divide pasta among bowls or transfer to one large family-style serving bowl and top with parsley/garlic mixture and more crushed red pepper, if desired.

Peking Pork Chops

Believe it or not, my family, who is originally from Little Italy and Chinatown in downtown Manhattan made some of the most authentic Chinese Food I have ever had. Since they had access to all the best Chinese restaurants and grocery stores on Mott, Mulberry and Baxter Streets, when they took a break from cooking Italian, they brought their A for Asian food game. My mom's spare ribs and hoisin chicken and my Aunt Faye's fried rice were second to none. These Peking pork chops, which are the perfect blend of sweet and spicy, will have you making a large vat of extra sauce, just to pour over the rice (I've also made cauliflower rice as a low carb option and it's just as delicious). With one bite, your family will think twice about grabbing that take out menu. The sweet and spicy Asian-inspired flavors coupled with the tenderness and juiciness of the pork makes this a perfect dish to serve with fried rice or cau-LIE-flower "fried rice."

SERVINGS: 4 | Prep Time: 20 minutes | Cooking Time: 30 minutes

INGREDIENTS:
2 pounds of boneless loin pork chops (1/2" thick, pounded if prefered)
2 large eggs for marinade
2 tablespoons of corn starch for marinade
1 tablespoon of rice wine vinegar for marinade
1 teaspoon of salt for marinade
3 tablespoons of ketchup for sauce
1 tablespoon of oyster sauce for sauce
1 tablespoon of chili sauce for sauce
1 tablespoon of hoisin sauce for sauce
2 tablespoons of Worcestershire sauce for sauce
3 tablespoons of rice wine vinegar for sauce
3 tablespoons of brown sugar for sauce
4 tablespoons of water for sauce
2 teaspoons of toasted sesame seeds, for garnish for sauce
2 chopped scallions, for garnish for sauce
1/4 cup of vegetable oil and 2 teaspoons of sesame oil, combined for frying

DIRECTIONS:
1. In a large bowl, mix together the marinade ingredients. Add the pork chops and toss to completely coat. Cover and marinade for 30 minutes.

2. Meanwhile in a separate bowl, prepare the sauce by whisking together all of the sauce ingredients in a bowl except for the scallions and sesame seeds. You may tweak it by adding more or less sugar, hoisin or chili sauce to your liking. Set aside.

3. Heat up a wok or a non-stick deep skillet with enough vegetable oil, over medium heat, deep fry the pork chops for 6-8 minutes total (approximately 3 minutes on each side) or until color changes to golden brown and slightly crispy. You can add a little bit of oil after each batch and may not use up the entire 1/4 cup of oil. Dish up, drain with paper towels and set aside.

4. Once all of the pork has been fried and set aside, pour the sauce into the skillet or wok. Bring the sauce to a quick boil over medium heat.

5. Transfer the cooked and drained pork chops back into the skillet or wok and toss well to coat both sides of the pork chops with the sauce. Continue to cook until the sauce has thickened. Plate the chops and sprinkle with the toasted sesame seeds and chopped scallions. Serve immediately.

Dani's "Too Vodka-ing Simple" Arrabbiata Vodka Sauce

Rachel Ray called it "You Won't be Single for Long" Penne alla Vodka; Chic East Hampton restaurant Nick and Toni's has had in on its menu for over 20 years; model Gigi Hadad's recipe became one of the most googled topics, and the legendary Ina Garten reintroduced it as Penne alla Vecchia Bettola, sparking immense popularity. What is it about Vodka Sauce that makes it one of the most sought after Italian-American pasta dishes of all time? Is it because it contains alcohol? or that it's so amazingly creamy and bright, super quick and comes together in 30 minutes? Is it that it's meatless, and is made with simple ingredients that we probably already have at home? Probably all of the above. This will be your go-to vodka sauce recipe that is the perfect weeknight meal for busy nights or for a family Sunday dinner, and if you do not attempt to make it, then I really don't know what the vodka is wrong with you.

SERVINGS: 8 | Prep Time: 15 minutes | Cooking Time: 40 minutes

INGREDIENTS:
6 tablespoons of extra virgin olive oil
2 medium sweet onions, chopped
5 minced garlic cloves
1/2 teaspoon red pepper flakes
2- 28-ounce cans of crushed tomatoes
2/3 cup of vodka
2 tablespoons of tomato paste
2 tablespoons of balsamic vinegar
2 teaspoons of sea salt
1/2 cup of fresh chopped basil
1 cup of heavy cream
1/2 cup of half and half
5 tablespoons of grated Parmigiano-Reggiano cheese plus more for serving
Fresh black pepper, to taste
1 pound of pasta

DIRECTIONS:
1. In a large sauté pan, sauté the onions and garlic over medium heat as you normally would until translucent, then add the red pepper and stir.

2. Stir in the crushed tomatoes and vodka and continue cooking that for 5-7 minutes until reduced a bit, while stirring to prevent it from sticking.

3. Add the paste, balsamic, salt and pepper to taste. Reduce the heat to low simmer and partially cover for about 20-25 minutes or until the volume is reduced by half, while giving it an occasional stir.

4. Stir in the heavy cream, half and half and basil. Cook until it is warmed through about 2-3 minutes.

5. Stir in the cheese.

6. Separately boil the pasta. This will be enough sauce for about 2+ pounds of pasta. Add more cheese for serving with additional basil, if desired.

Chicken Marsala with Creamy Polenta

Arguably one of the most sought after traditional Italian-American dishes served in restaurants, once you make this next level but simple recipe of golden pan-fried chicken cutlets and mushrooms on a bed of creamy polenta swimming in a rich Marsala wine sauce at home, you'll have to have a Plan B next time you dine out.

═══════════════ ✗ ═══════════════

SERVINGS: 4 | Prep Time: 15 minutes | Cooking Time: 30 minutes

INGREDIENTS:

1-1/2 pounds boneless skinless chicken breasts, pounded ¼-inch thick or chicken tenderloins

4 tablespoons of all-purpose flour

1 teaspoon of kosher salt, plus more to taste

Pinch of black pepper, plus more to taste

1 tablespoon of extra virgin olive oil

3 tablespoons of unsalted butter, divided

8 ounces of sliced bella or button mushrooms

1 medium shallot, finely chopped

2 cloves of garlic, minced

2/3 cup of chicken broth

2/3 cup of dry Marsala wine

2/3 cup of heavy cream

2 teaspoons of chopped fresh thyme

2 tablespoons of chopped fresh Italian parsley, for serving

DIRECTIONS:

1. Place the flour, 1 teaspoon salt, and 1/2 teaspoon pepper in a zipper bag. Add the chicken to the bag; seal bag tightly and shake to coat the chicken. Set aside.

2. Over medium to high heat in a large skillet, heat the oil and 3 tablespoons of the butter in a large stainless-steel skillet. Stainless steel pans are the best for browning. Before you place the flour-coated chicken in the pan, shake off any excess flour and cook, turning once, until the chicken is golden on both sides and just barely cooked through, about 5 to 6 minutes total. Transfer the chicken to a plate and set aside.

3. Melt the remaining tablespoon of butter in the pan. Add the mushrooms and cook until the mushrooms begin to brown, 3 to 4 minutes, while stirring frequently so they do not burn or stick. Add the shallots, garlic, and a pinch of salt; cook for 1 to 2 minutes more. Add the broth, Marsala, heavy cream, thyme and 1/8 teaspoon of red pepper. With a wooden spoon, scrape any brown bits from the pan into the liquid. Bring the liquid to a boil, then reduce the heat to medium and gently boil, uncovered, until the sauce becomes thicker and darkened, and is reduced by about half, about 10 to 15 minutes. The goal is a thin cream sauce which will start to get toward the desired consistency toward the very end of the cooking time. Add the chicken and any juices that may have accumulated with it, back to the pan. Reduce the heat to simmer until the chicken is warmed through and the sauce thickens a bit more, 2 to 3 minutes. Sprinkle with parsley and serve.

Creamy Polenta: Makes 4 cups | Prep time: 10 minutes | Cooking time: 30 minutes

INGREDIENTS:

1 cup of course grain polenta

1 cup of grated Parmigiano-Reggiano cheese

4 tablespoons of unsalted butter

4 tablespoons of fine sea salt

Kosher salt and black pepper to taste

3 cups of water

2 cups of whole milk plus 1/2 cup or more of half and half

DIRECTIONS:

1. Bring milk and 3 cups water to a boil over medium-high heat in a medium saucepan. Reduce heat to medium. Gradually add polenta, whisking constantly until there are no lumps then bring to a simmer. Reduce heat to low, cover pan, and cook, whisking every 10–15 minutes, until thickened and no longer gritty, 30–35 minutes. Remove from heat and add Parmigiano, butter, and salt and pepper. Cook, whisking, until butter and cheese are melted, and polenta is the consistency of porridge, adding half and half as needed, about 1 minute.

2. Polenta can be made a few hours ahead. Store covered at room temperature. Do not refrigerate. Reheat over medium-low, adding milk as needed to soften.

Squid Ink Pasta (Linguine al Nero di Seppia)

Pasta with Squid Ink is one of the most unique and dramatic dishes in Sicilian cuisine, given its black color. Because of its refined taste and tangy sea flavor, it is often a prized menu item at many top-notch restaurants. I'd venture to say that many people, Italian and non-Italian alike, have not tried squid ink, and if they have, very many have not tried making squid ink pasta at home. There is squid-ink pasta, in which the squid ink is mixed into the dough so that the pasta itself is jet black, but that is a different dish. In this recipe, regular pasta is used and tossed in a tangy sauce consisting of the actual squid ink. It is really worth getting familiar with. The taste is earthy and silky, salty and paired with garlic, oil, crushed red pepper and squid, it is a magical culinary adventure. As equally rustic as it is sophisticated, this pasta is perfect for a romantic evening at home or for a dinner party when paired with a cold Lugana or Chardonnay wine.

SERVINGS: 4 | Prep Time: 30 minutes | Cooking Time: 100 minutes

INGREDIENTS:

1 1/2 pounds of fresh, uncleaned squid
(if you are unable to obtain squid with the ink sacs, you may purchase the packets of cuttlefish ink and use 1 packet for this recipe).
1/2 cup of extra virgin olive oil
3 cloves of peeled, minced garlic
1 small bunch of minced flat leaf Italian parsley
Freshly ground black pepper, to taste
2 tablespoons of tomato paste, diluted with a little water
1/3 cup of dry white wine
1-2 tablespoons of coarse sea salt, plus more for seasoning to taste
1 pound of nero di seppia (or regular) linguine, depending if you prefer a more traditional taste
Fine sea salt, to taste
Crushed red pepper, to taste, if desired

DIRECTIONS:

1. Rinse the squid well under cold water and clean the squid by separating the heads from the tentacles. Remove the guts and set aside the ink sacs, leaving them intact.

2. Slice the bodies into thin rings and chop the tentacles. Over a small bowl, open the ink sacs, collect the ink and set aside.

3. In a large deep skillet, heat the oil and sauté the garlic until golden in color, careful not to burn.

4. Add the squid, parsley and a generous quantity of freshly ground black pepper.

5. Cover and simmer the sauce over low heat for about 45 minutes, checking and stirring periodically to ensure that the squid is not sticking to the bottom of the pan, adding a little hot water if necessary.

6. Once the sauce has simmered, mix in the paste and white wine.

7. Simmer uncovered for about 15-20 minutes.

8. Dilute the sauce with about 1/2 cup of hot water or more if necessary. Cover and simmer for about 30 more minutes. By this point, the sauce should not be too soupy or too dry. If you were unable to use squid containing ink sacs, add the separate packages of cuttlefish ink into the saucepan. Otherwise, add the ink you collected from the squid into the sauce, adding the amount that you desire, and mix thoroughly.

9. Bring a salted pot of water to rapid boil. Cook the pasta al dente according to package instructions, usually 8-10 minutes, straining well.

10. Toss the linguine with the sauce to coat evenly. Serve and enjoy, garnishing with crushed red pepper if desired.

Sunday Sauce and Meatballs

If I had $1 for everyone who asked me if I was going to include this in my cookbook, I would almost have as much money as I had from everyone saying that their mother, grandmother, nonna, or nana, made the best Sunday sauce. Sunday sauce and meatballs fulfills a need so basic, so primal, that it needs no introduction. In law, we call it Res Ipsa Loquitur, Latin for "that which speaks for itself." Everyone has their own way of making Sunday sauce, and of course, everyone believes theirs is the best. I once read a funny saying: "If an Italian lady invites you over to eat at her house, she either really likes you or she just wants to show you that her sauce is better than yours." For my non-Italian friends who have never made this: this one is for you. For my Italian friends, I won't be offended if you skip this one and turn the page, in fact, I'd expect it and probably do the same to you! Ha!

SERVINGS: 30-40 meatballs | Prep Time: 15 minutes | Cooking Time: 1 hour

INGREDIENTS FOR MEATBALLS:

1 pound of ground beef
1 pound of ground veal
1 1/2 cups of Italian seasoned breadcrumbs, preferably homemade
3/4 cup of freshly grated Pecorino Romano cheese
1 1/2 cups of cooled tomato sauce
2 cloves of garlic, peeled and finely minced

1 pound of ground pork
5 eggs, beaten
2 teaspoons of Kosher salt
Black pepper, to taste
3 tablespoons of chopped Italian parsley
Vegetable, canola or grapeseed oil, for frying

DIRECTIONS:

1. With gloved hands, gently combine all ingredients together in a large bowl (except the oil) and shape meatballs into a little bit larger than a golf ball size (2-3 inches) and lay them on parchment paper, careful not to overwork the meat.

2. Heat the oil over medium heat in a large sauce pan or deep skillet over until the oil is very hot but not smoking.

3. Brown the meatballs in batches over medium to high heat. When the bottom half of the meatball is very brown and slightly crisp, gently with tongs, turn and cook the top half, several minutes on each side until cooked fully. Drain on paper towels and set aside.

*Some people just brown the meatballs and allow them to cook fully in the sauce - however, if you like plain fried meatballs, as my family and I do (we don't put them all in the sauce), you would fry them until fully cooked inside.

INGREDIENTS FOR SAUCE:

1 pound of lean, bone-in pork chops (or you can use braciole, short ribs, spare ribs or whatever combination of meat you prefer)
1 pound of veal shoulder, cut into chunks
1/2-pound hot Italian sausage with fennel
3 cans of 28-ounce crushed San Marzano tomatoes
2 small onions, chopped
2 cups of fresh basil
1 teaspoon of salt
1 cup of extra virgin olive oil

1/2 pound of beef chuck meat, cubed
1/2 pound of sweet Italian sausage
1 cup of dry red wine
3 cloves of garlic, chopped
2 teaspoons of red pepper flakes
1 teaspoon of black pepper

1. Season all meat cubes with salt and pepper. In a large pot over medium heat, heat some of the oil and sear the veal and beef cubes separately until browned. As you don't want to overcrowd the meat, you will do this step in batches so they will get a nice brown crust. Transfer them to a plate. Don't worry if the meat is not cooked through because it will finish cooking in the sauce.
2. Brown the pork chops in the same pan over medium heat, about 10 minutes, adding extra oil if necessary. Transfer to a plate.
3. Over the same medium heat, do the same with the sausages by themselves, adding extra oil as necessary, browning on each side. Transfer to a plate. Again, don't worry if the sausage is not cooked through, as they will finish cooking while in the sauce.
4. In the same pot, over medium heat, deglaze the pan by adding 1/2 cup of dry red wine and scraping up the bits at the bottom with a flat edge wooden spoon.
5. Add the chopped onion and another tablespoon of olive oil and saute about 2 minutes until they are soft and lightly browned, scraping the bottom of the pot with the wooden spoon, loosening up any stuck brown bits. Add the garlic and crushed red pepper and cook about a minute or two, until golden, careful not to burn it.
6. Add the remaining 1/2 cup of red wine and cook until the mixture is reduced by half. Add the tomatoes and simmer on low heat for 1 hour.
7. Add the veal, beef, sausage, pork chops and some meatballs to the tomato sauce and simmer for minimum 1 hour more over low heat, the longer the better.
8. In a separate large pot of salted boiling water, cook the pasta al dente according to package instructions. Drain the pasta, toss it with the sauce and serve immediately.

Lemon Saffron Risotto with Shrimp and Peas

This creamy shrimp risotto spiked with saffron is a must do on an Italian menu. The flavors scream spring and summer but if lemon is also your love language, you will not dream waiting that long to make this. The pairing of the plump shrimp, with fresh spring peas and the chewiness of the lemony rice will take center stage as one of your go-to risotto recipes that the whole family will love.

SERVINGS: 4 | Prep Time: 35 minutes | Cooking Time: 25 minutes

INGREDIENTS:
4 cups of chicken broth
2 cups of water
1 teaspoon of lemon zest and 5 teaspoons of lemon juice
Sea Salt and freshly ground pepper, to taste
2 tablespoons of extra virgin olive oil and more for drizzling
1 cup of diced small yellow onion
1 1/2 cups of Arborio rice
1/4 cup of dry white wine (I use Chardonnay)
1 pinch of saffron
1 pound of large peeled deveined shrimp
1 cup of peas
3 tablespoons of unsalted butter at room temperature
3/4 cup of grated Parmigiano-Reggiano and more for serving

DIRECTIONS:
1. In a saucepan, combine chicken broth, water, lemon zest, 1 1/4 teaspoons of salt and 1/4 teaspoon of pepper together. Bring to a simmer in a large skillet over medium heat.

2. Meanwhile, heat a large skillet over medium heat and add 2 tablespoons of olive oil, and sauté the onion with salt until translucent, about 5 minutes.

3. Add the rice and cook for about 3 to 4 minutes then add the wine and saffron and cook until mostly evaporated, about 30 seconds.

4. Keep ladling one cup of the broth mixture into the skillet until most of the broth is absorbed every few minutes. Stir continuously and slowly, while adding a cup of broth at a time. Risotto should be finished when it's al dente at about 20 minutes or so.

5. Last step is adding the shrimp and peas with the leftover broth. Careful not to overcook the shrimp or they will be too chewy - just until they are pink. Remove from heat and grate the cheese and add the butter and lemon juice. If you're not serving right away and the risotto absorbs much of the moisture (Arborio rice tends to do this) just add more broth.

Beef Bolognese Sauce (Ragù alla Bolognese)

Italian comfort food in its rich, beefy splendor. There are many debates on what an authentic Bolognese sauce consists of. The native region from which it derives is the Bologna region of Italy, arguably the epicenter of traditional Italian cuisine. Although the Accademia Italiana della Cucina, the authority for Italian cuisine, officially registered a Bolognese recipe with the Bologna Chamber of Commerce in 1982, many recipes abound and the debates on what should and should not be in a "Bolognese" sauce still exist. Some say that anything but the registered recipe should merely be considered a ragù and not a Bolognese (sort of like usage of the word "champagne" to describe a sparkling wine originating from outside the Champagne region of France). However, one thing remains constant in all the recipes, however minimally they may differ. All will agree that a good Bolognese (or ragù) takes time. Like many things in life, it will be well worth the wait. If you're looking for a quick dinner that comes together in 30 minutes, Bolognese sauce is not for you. If anyone tells you they make a good Bolognese in less than an hour, do not trust their palate or their ability to tell time. The sauce needs to simmer slowly so the flavors develop together and become richer. All the more reason as you're using vino for the recipe, to pour yourself a glass or two and enjoy the ride.

SERVINGS: 6 | Prep Time: 20 minutes | Cooking Time: 5 hours

INGREDIENTS:
2 tablespoons of vegetable oil
4 tablespoons of butter plus 1 tablespoon for tossing the pasta
2/3 cup of chopped onion
2/3 cup of chopped celery
2/3 cup of chopped carrots
1 pound of beef (or 1-part pork to 2 parts beef)
Kosher salt
Freshly milled black pepper
1 cup of milk or 1 cup of half and half (if you would like it richer)
1 - 28 ounce can of San Marzano whole tomatoes, crushed and cut up with juice, or if you prefer a less "saucy" Bolognese you can just use 1 - 6 ounce can of tomato paste instead of the whole tomatoes.
1/4 cup of flat-leaf Italian parsley
1 1/2 pounds of pasta, preferably tagliatelle
1/8 teaspoon of nutmeg
1 cup of dry white wine
Freshly grated Parmigiano-Reggiano, for serving

DIRECTIONS:
1. Put the oil, butter, and onion in a saucepan on a medium flame. Cook and stir the onion until translucent, about 5 minutes, then add the celery and carrots. Cook for about 2-3 minutes, stirring the vegetables to coat them well.

2. Add the meat and simultaneously a large pinch of Kosher salt and a few grindings of pepper. Crumble the meat with a fork and stir until it is browned and no red parts remain.

3. Add milk or half and half and let it simmer gently, stirring frequently until it has bubbled away, about 1 hour. Add nutmeg and stir.

4. Add wine and let it simmer until evaporated, about 1 hour more. Add the tomatoes and stir thoroughly. When the tomatoes bubble, lower the heat so the sauce simmers on the lowest possible flame. Cook uncovered for 3+ hours, stirring occasionally. While the sauce is cooking, it may begin to dry out and the fat separates from the actual meat so add a 1/2 cup of water when necessary, but in the end no water should be left when you serve it. Add salt and pepper to taste.

5. Toss with drained pasta, adding an additional tablespoon of butter and serve with grated Parmigiano-Reggiano on the side.

Chinatown-style "Take Out" Spare Ribs

Growing up, there was nothing like homemade pretend "take out" Chinese spare ribs. My family's famous Chinatown recipe, which has the ribs so tender they fall off the bone, always wows even the most diverse crowds. Perfect for bringing to a barbeque, a tailgate, or a pot luck with some steamed rice, your fortune reads: You will be asked for the spare rib recipe over and over again.

SERVINGS: 3-4 | Prep Time: 10-15 minutes (minimum 4-6 hours marinating) | Cooking Time: 75-90 minutes

INGREDIENTS:
1 rack of spare ribs (8-10 pounds) St. Louis-style work best, individually sliced into single ribs
1/2 cup of hoisin sauce
1/2 cup of soy sauce
4 tablespoons of dark brown sugar
4 tablespoons of honey
1 teaspoon of granulated garlic
2 tablespoons of orange juice
1 teaspoon of grated fresh ginger
1/2 teaspoon of paprika
1/2 tablespoon of 5 spice powder
5 tablespoons of ketchup
1 teaspoon of black pepper
1 teaspoon of red food coloring
2 scallions, for garnish

DIRECTIONS:
1. Mix all the marinade ingredients into medium bowl. Divide the ribs into 2 zipper bags and empty half of the bowl or marinade into each of them. Save a little bit of marinade for later. Either marinate the ribs overnight in the refrigerator or for 4-6 hours. The longer the ribs marinate the better.

2. Preheat oven to 350°F. Prepare a roasting pan lined with heavy duty foil for easy clean up. You can roast right on the foil but brush a little vegetable oil on the foil. Otherwise, if you have a roasting rack to place on top of the pan, you can add about 2 cups of water to the pan so there is about a half inch of water and place the spare ribs rib side up on the rack into the preheated oven.

3. Roast for 30 minutes covered with a tent of aluminum foil. Flip the ribs over and then roast for another 45-60 minutes, uncovered, watching and turning as necessary for even cooking. If you're using a roasting pan, replace the water as necessary if it dries up. Finish them under the broiler for 5-10 minutes so the ends are crispy. You can and should baste the ribs about 2-3 times with the reserved marinade while they are in the oven. Serve with sliced scallions on top.

Pasta with Crabs (Granchi alla Marinara)

My signature dish. A Napoletana Christmas Eve staple, we ate this every year as a first course as part of the Cena della Viglia feast, or as some call it, the Feast of the 7 Fishes. Best when made a whole day before you eat it, you may call this Southern Italian "Liquid Gold" by other names, or use spaghetti instead of linguine, but if you know it, you appreciate that the sweet flavor of this sauce is second to none. Convinced that blue crab sauce runs through my veins, I have no words to describe how amazing the smell of this sauce is bubbling on the stove. By no means a first date meal, be prepared to put on a bib and get down and dirty cracking the crabs. Getting to the claw meat makes this sauce all the more worth it. Mentally, each time I make it, I am transported to Christmas Eves past, when everyone was around the table, and times were simple. Isn't that what we all want from the dishes we make?

SERVINGS: 8-10 | Prep Time: 1 hour (including cleaning the crabs) | Cooking Time: 3 hours (for best results, refrigerate overnight and serve next day)

INGREDIENTS:
12 fresh large, cleaned blue claw crabs (preferably males) *
3 - 28-ounce cans of peeled San Marzano tomatoes
3 - 28-ounce cans of crushed San Marzano tomatoes
1 1/4 cups of extra virgin olive oil
9 cloves of garlic, peeled, smashed and minced
4 tablespoons of chopped flat leaf parsley
1 1/2 tablespoons (or more) of red pepper flakes, to taste
2 cups of fresh basil leaves, plus more for serving
Kosher salt
Freshly ground black pepper, to taste
2 pounds of linguine or spaghetti

DIRECTIONS:
1. Open the 6 tomato cans. Empty the contents of the 3 cans of peeled tomatoes into a large bowl. Crush the tomatoes by hand with clean hands or use a masher (I like them chunky, so I don't like to over crush).

2. Heat oil in an extra-large pot over medium to high heat. Once it's hot add the garlic and cook for a minute or two until it is fragrant and golden brown, but never burnt.

3. Add all the tomatoes into the pot of garlic and oil. Then add the parsley and red pepper flakes.

4. Turn the heat up high and add the crabs. When the sauce starts boiling, lower the heat to simmer and cook for about an hour, stirring occasionally. Add half the basil, stir more. Cook the sauce for about 3 hours on the lowest simmer possible. Add the rest of the basil right before serving.

5. When the sauce is ready, you can serve as is. But it's best to cool it down and then refrigerate overnight and eat it the next day so the crab flavor really penetrates the sauce.

6. When it's time to serve, bring a large pot of well-salted water to a boil (always salt the water after it boils or it will take longer). Add the linguine and cook it until al dente. Drain.

7. Place the pasta in a large serving bowl or platter. Pour the crab sauce over the pasta and you can scatter with more basil on top as well as black and/or red pepper. Serve with crabs on the side and lots of bread for dipping.

* Males, called "Jimmies," are generally larger and have a narrow, T-shaped "apron" on the back of their shell, while female crabs, called "Sooks," have a wide apron. In addition, live females have red-tipped claws, while male claws are blue. I like to say the females wear red nail polish. I prefer males for my sauce - meatier - but some like females because they say the sauce is "sweeter" from their roe. Whichever you choose, make sure you are getting fresh, not frozen, live blue claw crabs for the sauce. The less time spent after the crabs are killed and cleaned until they go into the sauce the better it is.

Lamb and Orzo Stuffed Peppers with Feta Cheese

There are tons of recipes for stuffed peppers out there and not many come close to my Nana's tried and true with breadcrumb and egg, except for this one. If you're looking for something different, when it comes to flavors, I looked to the Mediterranean for inspiration. Warm and savory ground lamb, spiced with cumin, coriander, chili and allspice combined with tangy lemon and feta, and fresh mint, brings this complexity of flavors that is unlike any stuffed pepper recipe I've ever encountered. Many different grains may be used in stuffed peppers: rice, couscous, breadcrumbs, bulgar or quinoa, but the smooth orzo paired perfectly with the lamb. The lamb orzo mixture stands alone as a delicious meal even by itself, and can be served warm or cold, with a squeeze of lemon. These stuffed peppers can be made ahead and baked just before serving which makes them a good choice when planning weeknight dinners.

SERVINGS: 2-3 | Prep Time: 10-15 minutes | Cooking Time: 45 minutes

INGREDIENTS:

6 bell peppers (any and all colors you like)
1 pound of ground lamb
1 teaspoon of sea salt or kosher salt
1 teaspoon of freshly ground black pepper
1 tablespoon of grapeseed, canola or vegetable oil
1 diced large yellow onion
5 cloves of minced garlic
8 ounces of orzo
Extra virgin olive oil
1 14.5 ounce can of diced tomatoes, drained
3/4 teaspoon of allspice, ground
1 1/4 teaspoon of ground cumin
1 1/4 teaspoon of ground chili powder
1 cup of finely chopped fresh parsley
1 cup of finely chopped fresh dill
1 cup of finely chopped fresh mint
2 tablespoons of lemon juice, freshly squeezed
8 ounces of feta or halloumi cheese cut into diced pieces
Parmigiano-Reggiano, optional for serving

DIRECTIONS:

1. Rinse the peppers and slice them lengthwise (cooks more evenly and easier to stuff and eat), removing the seeds and white pith with a paring knife. Add the grapeseed (or canola/vegetable oil) to a large skillet over a high flame then add the garlic, onion and salt and sauté until translucent. Then add the lamb and sauté for about 3-5 minutes, breaking up the meat into crumbles with a wooden spoon. Add the drained diced tomatoes and another 1/4 teaspoon of salt. Turn off the heat.

2. Boil the orzo in a separate salted pot of water. Undercook the orzo just about a minute less than al dente. When it is done, add 1/3 cup of the orzo water to the lamb skillet. Drain the orzo and return it to the pot it was previously in. Combine the lamb/tomato mixture into the pot with the orzo. Then add the spices: cumin, allspice, chili powder. Mix well.

3. Preheat the oven to 450°F. Arrange the peppers on a baking sheet lined with parchment paper. Drizzle or mist the peppers with the olive oil and sprinkle each with a pinch of salt. Bake for approximately 20 minutes. While the peppers are roasting, chop the dill, mint and parsley and combine into the lamb/orzo mixture along with the feta (or halloumi) and lemon juice. Stir and add more salt to taste, and the black pepper.

4. Remove peppers from oven and generously stuff each one with the lamb/orzo mixture. Drizzle or mist some olive oil on top of each one. If you have extra filling, you can enjoy it by itself or refrigerate it and use it up to 3 days later to make more peppers!). Return the peppers to the oven and roast for another 15 minutes until they look a bit charred and the cheese is melty. For serving I like to grate some Parmigiano-Reggiano on top but that's because I like it extra cheesy.

Pasta with Sardines and Fennel (Pasta Con Le Sarde e Finocchi)

This pasta is essentially Sicily in a bowl - it offers a true taste of traditional Sicilian cuisine. The unusual flavor combination of the sweet and savory sardines, fennel, pignoli nuts and raisins reflects the diverse past of this island, rich with history. Serve this up with a crisp, chilled glass of white wine and close your eyes, you could be in Palermo. This dish converts even the pickiest eaters who are not huge fans of sardines since the complexity and textures of the fennel, raisins and pine nuts serve to balance out the salty taste of the fish. It's one of my favorite dishes to make, especially on St. Joseph's Day, when many Italians also make it. Some say the toasted breadcrumbs are symbolic of the wood shavings of the carpenter that St. Joseph was. My son's middle name is Joseph, and being that he's half Sicilian, this is a saint, a day, and a dish that is near and dear to my heart.

SERVINGS: 4 | Prep Time: 15 minutes | Cooking Time: 45 minutes

INGREDIENTS:
2 pounds of sardines trimmed and deboned, yielding about 1 1/4 pounds, substitute large best-quality canned sardines, drained
3 tablespoons of tomato paste
3/4 cup of extra virgin olive oil
1/2 teaspoon of crushed red pepper
1/2 cup of golden raisins
1/2 cup of brown raisins or currants
1/2 cup of dry white wine
2 tablespoons of butter
1 cup of plain breadcrumbs
1 onion, finely chopped
2 minced garlic cloves
1 pound of fennel bulb, finely chopped, fronds chopped and reserved
1 tablespoon of crushed fennel seeds
1/4 cup of rinsed capers
Sea salt
Black pepper
Pinch of sugar
1/2 cup of toasted pignoli nuts
1 pound of bucatini pasta

DIRECTIONS:
1. In a small bowl, combine both sets of raisins (or raisins and currants) and crushed pepper and wine and set aside. Melt the butter in a small sauté pan until golden brown. Transfer to a bowl, stir in 2 tablespoons of the olive oil and set aside. Bring a large pot of salted water to a boil.

2. In a heavy skillet over medium-low heat, heat 1/2 cup of olive oil. When oil shimmers, add garlic, onion, fennel bulb, fennel seeds and tomato paste as well as salt to taste. Stir it occasionally until the fennel is tender, about 25 minutes.

3. Add the raisin-wine mixture and the sardines into the skillet, breaking them up slightly with a wooden spoon. Bring to a boil and gently simmer for about 10 minutes. If using canned sardines, you can add them in and cook for 3 minutes.

4. Boil the pasta until al dente according to package instructions, then strain and return to the pasta pot that it cooked in over low heat, reserving 1 cup of pasta water. Then add the fennel and sardine mixture. Add the remaining olive oil, capers, toasted pine nuts and fennel fronds, saving a few for garnish. Season with salt and pepper to taste. Add some reserved pasta water to keep everything moistened, salt and pepper, and a pinch of sugar.

5. In a small skillet, toast the breadcrumbs with 2 tablespoons of the olive oil until golden brown.

6. Divide the pasta among bowls and sprinkle each bowl with breadcrumbs and remaining fennel fronds over each. Serve immediately.

Eggplant Tomato and Basil "Rata-Louie"

Ratatouille, or rather, "Rata-Louie?" My eggplant, tomato and basil Italian twist on the French classic. Need I fill you in on the pesto drizzle with crusty heavily floured peasant bread for dipping? A no-meat Friday hardened habit, this is simply a delicious dish for eggplant lovers who are craving the parmesan-ish flavors who want an alternative to frying. A picturesque meal for entertaining, the layering of veggies is also a fun one to prep with kids as sous chefs.

SERVINGS: 6 | Prep Time: 15-20 minutes | Cooking Time: 60 minutes

INGREDIENTS FOR THE RATATOUILLE:
2 medium eggplants cut into rounds
2 large beefsteak tomatoes, cut into rounds
16-ounce fresh salted mozzarella, cut into rounds, strained or dried on paper towels for at least 15 minutes
1 bunch of fresh large basil leaves, washed and dried

INGREDIENTS FOR THE SAUCE:
1 - 28 ounce can of crushed San Marzano tomatoes
3 tablespoons of extra virgin olive oil
3 cloves of chopped garlic
1/4 cup of fresh basil, chopped
1 tablespoon of crushed red pepper
Salt, as needed
Black pepper, as needed

INGREDIENTS FOR THE HERB OIL:
1/2 cup tablespoons extra virgin olive oil
2 cloves garlic, minced
1/2 cup chopped basil leaves
1/4 teaspoon dried thyme
2 tablespoons of Pecorino Romano cheese
Salt, as needed
Black pepper, as needed

DIRECTIONS:
1. Preheat oven to 375°F. Warm up a 15" cast iron skillet over medium heat.

2. Heat up oil and sauté chopped garlic until golden brown. Add the crushed tomatoes, red pepper, salt and pepper.

3. Let the sauce simmer for about 10 minutes. Remove from heat and mix in the basil. Arrange the sliced veggies, and mozzarella over the sauce, alternating.

4. Mix the herb oil ingredients together (I pulse them in the blender) and drizzle on top of the veggies. Bake it in the oven for 40 minutes covered with aluminum foil, followed by 20 minutes uncovered. Cool and enjoy. Serve with crusty bread for dipping.

Crumbled Sausage over Creamy Polenta

This quick comforting ragù is a great way to change up pasta night and is the perfect fusion of Southern and Northern Italian cooking. It is essentially the recipe for my Nana's Sunday Sausage ragù, except the cheesy, creamy bowl of polenta provides the base for a blanket of hearty sausage ragù instead of pasta. Like any ragù, it tastes even better the following day. It also freezes well for a night you just want a quick plate of pasta so you'll find yourself tripling the recipe each time to have extras.

SERVINGS: 2-3 | Prep Time: 10 minutes | Cooking Time: 40 minutes

INGREDIENTS:

1 pound of mixed spicy and sweet Italian sausage with fennel, out of the casing
1/3 cup of dry white wine
1/4 cup of minced flat leaf parsley
2 tablespoons of tomato paste
14 ounces of San Marzano crushed tomatoes
1 bay leaf
1 sprig of fresh thyme
1/8 teaspoon of nutmeg
1/4 teaspoon of red pepper flakes
Parmigiano-Reggiano
2 tablespoons of extra virgin olive oil
1 peeled carrot, finely chopped
1 peeled celery stalk, finely chopped
1 onion, finely chopped
1 teaspoon of sea salt, divided
1/4 teaspoon of freshly ground black pepper

DIRECTIONS:

Make the ragù:
1. Heat the oil in a large deep skillet and when hot, add the onion, carrot and celery, 1/2 teaspoon of salt and pepper. Cook until the vegetables are soft, and onion is translucent, about 5 minutes. Add the sausage and the remaining 1/2 teaspoon of salt. Sauté until the sausage is browned and crumbly, breaking it up with a wooden spoon, about 10 minutes.
2. Pour in the white wine and scrape up any brown bits from the bottom of the pan. Cook until the wine is totally evaporated.
3. Add the tomato paste and mix well. Add the tomatoes and their juices, bay leaf, thyme and red pepper. Bring to a boil then reduce to simmer, stirring occasionally about 30 minutes. Before serving remove the bay leaf and thyme sprigs.

Creamy Polenta: Makes 4 cups | Prep time: 10 minutes | Cooking time: 30 minutes

INGREDIENTS:

1 cup of course grain polenta
1 cup of grated Parmigiano-Reggiano cheese
4 tablespoons of unsalted butter
4 tablespoons of fine sea salt
Kosher salt and black pepper to taste
3 cups of water
2 cups of whole milk plus 1/2 cup or more of half and half

DIRECTIONS:

1. Bring milk and 3 cups water to a boil over medium-high heat in a medium saucepan. Reduce heat to medium. Gradually add polenta, whisking constantly until there are no lumps then bring to a simmer. Reduce heat to low, cover pan, and cook, whisking every 10–15 minutes, until thickened and no longer gritty, 30–35 minutes. Remove from heat and add Parmigiano, butter, and salt and pepper. Cook, whisking, until butter and cheese are melted, and polenta is the consistency of porridge, adding half and half as needed, about 1 minute.

2. Polenta can be made a few hours ahead. Store covered at room temperature. Do not refrigerate. Reheat over medium-low, adding milk as needed to soften.

Linguine and Clams (Linguine alle Vongole)

Of all of the recipes in my repertoire, few shout "summer" more than a bowl of linguine and clams. This classic Napoletana dish encompasses all of the best feelings of the season. It's bright, fresh, and light yet comforting, casual and elegant. This is a meal to enjoy al fresco with the people you love and is sure to be a showstopper to anyone unfamiliar with it.

One of the most iconic Italian pasta dishes ever, Linguine alle Vongole can be prepared either "bianco" (white) or "rosso" (tomato-based), or with spaghetti or linguine. My family always made their's bianco, with white wine, plenty of fresh garlic, lemon juice, and a sprinkling of crushed red pepper.

SERVINGS: 4-6 | Prep Time: 10 minutes | Cooking Time: 20 minutes

INGREDIENTS:
3 pounds of vongole, littleneck or manila clams, cleaned (retain some shells for serving)
1/4 cup of extra virgin olive oil, plus more for serving
2 Tablespoons of unsalted butter, plus more for serving
1 pound of linguine
4-8 cloves of minced garlic (depending how intense you prefer the garlic flavor)
1-2 dried chilis
1 cup of dry white wine (one that you would actually drink)
2 wedges of fresh lemon, for serving plus one wedge for recipe
1-2 handfuls of fresh chopped flat leaf parsley
Kosher salt, to taste

DIRECTIONS:
1. In a deep skillet, sauté pan or braiser (at least 12 inches wide or larger) over medium heat, add olive oil and sauté garlic and red pepper, stirring until garlic is fragrant and bronzed, about 1-2 minutes.

2. Bring a large pot of salted water to boil and cook linguine until it's about a minute shy of al dente, about 8 minutes or according to package instructions (pasta will finish cooking in the clam sauce and should have a little bite to it).

3. To the sauté pan, add white wine, squeezed lemon juice, and clams, cover pan, and steam over medium-high heat until clamshells have opened, about 5-8 minutes. Keep an eye on them, gently shaking the pan occasionally and transfer the clams as they open into another bowl. For tender clams, it's important not to overcook. Cover the bowl of cooked clams with aluminum foil. Discard any clams that do not open after 10 minutes.

4. Before straining the linguine, reserve 1/2 to 1 cup of pasta water. When all of the clams are cooked and removed from the pan, whisk 3 tablespoons of butter into the simmering steaming liquid.

5. Add the strained linguine to the pan, tossing to coat. Cook for about 1-2 minutes, until linguine is al dente. The sauce should be brothy, but lightly clinging to the pasta. If the linguine appears dry at any point, stir in some of the reserved pasta water, as needed.

6. Stir the chopped parsley into the pasta. Season to taste with salt, additional red pepper flakes, and more lemon juice, if needed. At this point, you can either remove the clams from their shells and stir them into the pasta, or serve the pasta topped with the whole clams for guests to de-shell in their bowls, for a nicer presentation. I like to do half and half.

7. Garnish the dish with a drizzle of fruity olive oil, fresh lemon wedges, and the remaining parsley. Serve immediately.

Chicken Tikka Masala

You've been itching for a change recently. You know you want to shake things up, spice things up a bit, and throw a wrench into the proverbial weeknight dinner routine. Enter Chicken Tikka Masala. Being Italian-American, I am never short for having stockpiles of tomato sauce on hand in the pantry. All these years of it growing up, and I only recently had the epiphany that I was a couple of basic ingredients away from an amazing at-home complex-flavored Tikka Masala. The creamy yogurt helps tenderize the chicken and the garlic, coriander, ginger and spices in the tomato-based marinade infuse it with tons of flavor. Believe me, served with a side of Basmati rice, and there will quickly be naan left!

✕

SERVINGS: 4 | Prep Time: 15 minutes | Cooking Time: 30 minutes

INGREDIENTS FOR THE MARINADE:
2 pounds of boneless, skinless chicken breasts, cut into bite sized chunks (many recipes call for thighs, but I prefer breast meat)

1 cup of plain full fat yogurt (not greek)
1 tablespoon of minced ginger
2 teaspoons of garam masala
1 teaspoon of ground cumin
1 tablespoon of fresh squeezed lemon juice
1 teaspoon of Kosher salt

1 1/2 cups of minced garlic
1 teaspoon of ground turmeric
1 teaspoon of paprika
1 teaspoon of celery seed
1/2 teaspoon of ground red chili powder
1 teaspoon of black pepper

INGREDIENTS FOR THE SAUCE:
2 tablespoons of vegetable or canola oil
2 small yellow onions or 1 large onion, finely chopped
1 tablespoon of minced ginger
1 1/2 teaspoons of ground cumin
1 teaspoon of ground coriander
2 teaspoons of ground red chili powder (or more if you prefer)
1 teaspoon of black pepper
6 tablespoons or more of fresh cilantro to garnish

2 tablespoons of salted butter
1 1/2 tablespoons of minced garlic
1 1/2 teaspoons of garam masala
1 teaspoon of ground turmeric
14 ounces of tomato passata
1 teaspoon of Kosher salt
1 1/4 cups of heavy cream
2 teaspoons of brown sugar

DIRECTIONS:
1. In a large mixing bowl, combine the chicken and all ingredients for marinade. Mix together and let marinate for at least 30 minutes to overnight if you can. The longer the better, especially for the breasts, which I marinate overnight for optimal tenderizing.

2. On a medium to high heat, heat the oil in a cast iron large skillet. When it is hot, add the chicken pieces in small batches of 3 or 4, making sure not to overcrowd. Brown them about 3 minutes on each side (don't worry if they don't seem fully cooked - they will continue cooking in the sauce). Set aside.

3. Melt the butter in the same pan. If it is too burnt, then use another pan. Sauté the onions until translucent, about 5 minutes, scraping up any brown bits on the bottom of the pan.

4. Add the minced garlic and ginger, and sauté for 1-2 minutes, then add the garam masala, turmeric, cumin and coriander. Sauté for about 30 seconds, while occasionally stirring.

5. Pour in the tomato passata, chili powder, salt and pepper. Simmer for 10-15 minutes, stirring occasionally until the sauce thickens and becomes a deep brownish reddish color.

6. Add the heavy cream and brown sugar and stir. Add the chicken and its juices back into the pan and cook for an additional 8-10 minutes until the chicken is cooked and the sauce is thick and bubbling. Pour in water if you feel it is necessary to thin it out.

7. Garnish with cilantro and serve with basmati rice or warm naan bread.

Lamb Bolognese Sauce

For the hypertechnical folk, I suppose this is a misnomer and should simply be called a Lamb ragù, since nothing outside the Accademia Italiana della Cucina can technically be considered a Bolognese, but most people refer to things colloquially these days, and I welcome any such people bringing this to my attention as I am flattered that you're actually reading my cookbook! I digress. I suppose this could be considered a fusion dish of sorts in that it incorporates lamb, an atypical meat to use in a traditional ragù and is perfect for Easter Sunday. The result is a deep intense flavor of lamb that sets this sauce apart from other classic meat sauces. Pair with a glass of Montepulciano d'Abruzzo and you will definitely be checking another box off of your culinary bucket list.

✕

SERVINGS: 4-6 | Prep Time: 10-15 minutes | Cooking Time: 1 - 1 1/2 hours

INGREDIENTS:

1 ground lamb shoulder
1 cup of milk or 1 cup half and half (if you would like it richer)
1 1/2 pounds of pasta
3 tablespoons of extra virgin olive oil
2 tablespoons of butter plus 1 tablespoon for tossing the pasta
1 tablespoon of extra virgin olive oil
2/3 cup of finely chopped red onion
2/3 cup of finely chopped celery
1/4 cup grated Parmigiano-Reggiano, for serving

1 cup of finely chopped carrots
2 cloves of minced garlic
1/8 teaspoon of nutmeg
1 bay leaf
1 1/2 cups of dry red wine
Kosher salt
Freshly milled black pepper
Pinch of chili flakes, plus more for serving
Fresh torn mint leaves, optional, for serving

12 ounce can of San Marzano whole tomatoes, crushed and cut up with juice OR if you prefer a less "saucy" bolognese you can just use 1 - 6 ounce can of tomato paste instead of the whole tomatoes

DIRECTIONS:

1. Add the olive oil, butter, and onion to a saucepan or Dutch oven over a medium flame. Cook and stir the onion until translucent and aromatic, then add the celery and carrots with a pinch of Kosher salt. Cook for about 3-4 minutes, stirring the vegetables to coat them well.

2. Add the lamb meat, a large pinch of Kosher salt and a few grindings of pepper. Crumble the meat with a fork or wooden spoon and stir until it is browned.

3. Add milk or half and half and let it simmer gently, stirring frequently until it has bubbled away. Add nutmeg and bay leaf and stir.

4. Add the wine and let it simmer until evaporated. Add the tomatoes and stir thoroughly. When the tomatoes bubble, lower the heat so the sauce simmers on the lowest possible flame. Cook uncovered, stirring occasionally, until the liquid is reduced to about half, about 1 1/2-2 hours. Scrape any bits up from the bottom of the pan when stirring. While the sauce is cooking, it may begin to dry out and the fat separates from the actual meat so add a little water when necessary, but in the end no water should be left when you serve it. Add salt and pepper to taste. Remove bay leaf when ready to serve.

5. Bring a large pot of salted water to boil. When the pasta is cooked al dente, remove and set aside 1/2 cup of the pasta water. Drain the pasta.

6. Toss the ragù with the drained pasta, adding an additional tablespoon of butter and 1 tablespoon of extra virgin olive oil and the reserved pasta water, tossing until the butter is melted and fully incorporated, and serve with grated Parmigiano-Reggiano, crushed red pepper and fresh torn mint, if desired.

Nana's Meatloaf (Polpettone)

Yes, my Napoletana Nana made meatloaf, but not the brown gravy and mashed potatoes kind of meatloaf that some of my friends had growing up. Italians call meatloaf polpettone, or "big meatball," which, in reality, is what it is. It's pretty much the same delicious mixture that she used to make for her Sunday meatballs, and it was stuffed with gooey mozzarella, topped with tomato sauce and baked in the oven. Every time I make it, I'm instantly teleported to the days of yesteryear. I know Nana would be so proud to know that her polpettone made it to these pages. Typically, she would serve it with a big salad.

SERVINGS: 4-6 | Prep Time: 15 minutes | Cooking Time: 45-60 minutes

INGREDIENTS:

2 pounds of ground beef (and/or pork, in equal amounts) (my Nana only used beef)
3/4 cup of grated Parmigiano-Reggiano cheese
2 tablespoons of Pecorino Romano Cheese
4 tablespoons of cold marinara sauce, preferably homemade (see my recipe for basic marinara sauce), plus more for serving.
2 large eggs
3-4 cloves of finely minced garlic
2 large slices of Italian bread, soaked in seltzer, squeezed dry and shredded
2 tablespoons of finely chopped Italian parsley
Sea salt and freshly ground black pepper, to taste
1 ball of salted fresh mozzarella, sliced, dried and strained on paper towels for at least 15 minutes

DIRECTIONS:

1. Preheat oven to 400°F. Combine all ingredients in a large bowl, mixing with your hands thoroughly, until you have an evenly incorporated mixture.

2. Fill a 9"x5" greased meatloaf pan from end to end halfway to the top with the mixture and flatten with your hands.

3. Add slices of the mozzarella from end to end on top of the meatloaf.

4. Layer the remaining meat mixture on top of the mozzarella. Coat the top of the meatloaf with a basting brush or back of the spoon with tomato sauce for color.

5. Bake for 45-60 minutes until the top is browned. An instant read thermometer should register 160°F in the middle of the meatloaf. Remove meatloaf from the oven and let it rest for about 10 minutes to settle. Serve the polpettone whole, directly from the baking dish or slice it on a serving platter. Many people also serve this with roasted potatoes. There are also other varieties of this with different types of cheeses like scarmoza, the addition of pignoli nuts, or hard-boiled eggs, but we only had it the way I wrote it above.

Napoletana Pizza Dough

Patience is certainly a virtue, and the best way I learned that was with this pizza dough recipe. Being a typical New Yorker, I never had patience to wait for anything to ferment over 24 hours, but this is one instance in which the old adage, it will be worth the wait, holds true. It's really such a simple and foolproof process, doesn't require any special equipment (I prefer to make it with my hands, but you can use a stand mixer) and the most difficult part is just planning ahead 72 hours. So if you think you are going to make pizza on a Saturday, just start making your dough on Wednesday. Yes, you can take it out prematurely, but the flavor really develops with a long fermentation. And yes, it can be frozen.

SERVINGS: makes about 4 - 10" pizzas or 3 - 12" pizzas*

INGREDIENTS:
500 grams of Type 00 Flour (I like Mulino Caputo® Chef's Flour or Tony Gemignani 00 Flour from Central Milling)
360 grams of room temperature filtered water (72% hydration)
16 grams of fine sea salt
16 grams of honey
1 gram of active dry yeast (you can use fresh yeast also. To convert from fresh yeast to active dry yeast, multiply the fresh quantity by 0.33).

*According to AVPN (Associazione Verace Pizza Napoletana) Regulations, Vera Pizza Napoletana is roundish, with a diameter of minimum 22 centimeters and maximum 35 centimeters, or 13.78", which presents a raised crust or "cornicone," swollen and free from burns, 1-2 centimeters, and must be soft and fragrant. The dough balls must weigh between 200 and 280 grams.

DIRECTIONS:
1. In a large bowl, add the flour and salt and whisk thoroughly.

2. Measure about 1/4 cup of water (approx 60 grams) and heat up in a microwave-safe cup or bowl or over the stove for about 10-15 seconds. Active dry yeast must be hydrated in warm (not hot) water before being incorporated into a dough. The water should be between 100°F and 110°F. If the water is too hot it can kill the yeast. Mix the yeast into the warm water and stir vigorously until it is dissolved, about 15 seconds. Set it aside for about 10 minutes. You can mix the honey into the yeast mixture at this point if you like because sugar actually helps to activate the yeast or you can opt to mix it later right into the dough.

3. Once the yeast is activated, slowly pour the yeast mixture into the flour and mix thoroughly with a wooden spoon or rubber spatula. Slowly, then pour the remaining room temperature water (300 grams), a little bit at a time, into the flour mixture and mix it thoroughly before pouring more in. Scrape the sides of the bowl and get that flour and water all incorporated. Add the honey and mix it until it's fully incorporated.

4. Dump the mixture onto the counter and rigorously knead the dough with your hands for about 3-4 minutes until all the clumps of flour are worked out. The dough will be sticky, just keep working it. If you need to wash off your hands with just water, do so but keep in mind when you do this and don't dry them you are adding more hydration to the dough, which isn't necessarily a bad thing. Sometimes I use a little olive oil on my hands. You don't have to.

5. Place the dough back into the large bowl and cover it tightly with plastic wrap. Make sure that it has enough room to double in size.

6. Leave the bowl out on the counter for 24 hours. After 24 hours, put the bowl in the refrigerator with the plastic wrap still on. Make sure it's not in the back of the refrigerator where it has the tendency to get too cold and frost. Leave the dough in the refrigerator for 3 days (72 hours). You can take it out and use it after having fermented for only 1 day or even 2 days but it will be at peak performance in terms of taste and texture at 3 days. You can use it past 3 days but no longer than 6 days.

7. When you remove the bulk dough from the refrigerator you will need to "ball up" your dough. Usually I cut the dough in 3 or 4 equal parts and make 250-280 gram dough balls. It depends what size pizza you would like to make. I store them in covered containers in the refrigerator (take-out pint or quart size soup containers are ideal for this since they stack easily).

8. After you make your dough balls, refrigerate them and remove them from the refrigerator at least 2-3 hours before baking your pizza so they get down to room temperature. I highly recommend preheating a Baking Steel® for 1 hour at 500°F before launching your pizza.

*Do women belong in the kitchen? Absolutely.
So do men. And children. It's the 21st
century, everyone belongs in the kitchen.*

Sometimes in life, you just have to work with what you have. Keep it simple.

Sides

Stuffed Mushrooms

Who doesn't love stuffed mushrooms? Baby bella mushrooms stuffed with mouth-watering garlicky, herby breadcrumbs and plenty of cheese. These are a staple when we're home for the holidays (although they do travel really well) and just about any time we have a crowd to entertain. The beautiful thing is that you can prep and stuff them ahead of time and bake them when you need them.

SERVINGS: 8 | Prep Time: 15 minutes | Cooking Time: 30 minutes

INGREDIENTS:
1 1/2 pound of baby bella mushrooms
2 tablespoons of unsalted butter
2 cloves of minced garlic
1/2 cup of seasoned breadcrumbs
Kosher salt, to taste
Freshly ground black pepper, to taste
1/4 cup of freshly grated Parmigiano-Reggiano, and more for serving
4 tablespoons of mayonnaise or 4 ounces of softened cream cheese
2 tablespoons of freshly chopped parsley and extra for serving

DIRECTIONS:
1. Preheat the oven to 400°F. Grease a baking sheet with brushed olive oil. Carefully remove stems from mushrooms and roughly chop the stems. Place the mushroom caps on the baking sheet.

2. In a medium skillet over medium heat, melt the butter, adding chopped mushroom stems and sauté for a few minutes until all the moisture is dissolved. Fold in the garlic and cook until fragrant, approximately 1-2 minutes. Add the breadcrumbs and let toast slightly, about 2-3 minutes. Season with salt and pepper, to taste. Remove from the heat and allow to cool slightly.

3. In a large bowl, mix together the mushroom stem mixture, the mayonnaise (or cream cheese), parsley and Parmigiano-Reggiano. Season with salt and pepper to taste. Fill the mushroom caps with filling and sprinkle with extra freshly grated Parmigiano-Reggiano.

4. Bake until the mushrooms are soft and the tops are golden-brown, about 20 minutes.

5. Garnish with parsley and serve.

Roasted Honey-glazed Brussels Sprouts with Pancetta

Crispy brussels sprouts are good, but crispy brussels sprouts with pancetta? That's pure heaven. The Italian distant cousin of bacon, the salty fat of pancetta melts over the sprouts as they roast, imparting its luscious porky flavor. For optimum caramelization, be sure to have the sprouts cut side lay flat against the pan. As they roast, the sprouts will get crispy and infused with the pancetta flavor. The result is a golden-brown exterior and tender inside. The toasted pignoli nuts add another dimension of both texture and flavor and the generous sweet chili-infused honey after roasting balances out the saltiness, ensuring this recipe will be a go-to holiday side dish for years. One chef's tip - double the recipe!

SERVINGS: 2 | Prep Time: 10 minutes | Cooking Time: 20 minutes

INGREDIENTS:
1 box fresh brussels sprouts
2 garlic cloves
2 tablespoons of extra virgin olive oil
1 cup of diced pancetta
1/2 cup of pignolis nuts
2 tablespoons of chili-infused or regular honey
salt & pepper

DIRECTIONS:
1. Rinse and cut the brussels sprouts in half, cutting off the bottom as well.

2. Chop the garlic finely. In a skillet sauté the garlic in olive oil then add the pancetta on a low to medium flame.

3. Add the sliced brussels sprouts. Toss around until they're browned, turn them over so they're roasted face down, about 5-7 minutes. While they're browning add in the pignoli nuts, salt and pepper to taste.

4. Just before removing from heat add the honey and toss around. Drizzle additional honey for serving if desired.

Crispy Fried Zucchini

Some have chips and dip, we have zucchini and dip. Who doesn't love crispy and cheesy fried zucchini from the abundant garden or the farmer's market? Sometimes, you are not looking for a full-blown parmesan but are still craving sauce. This dish brings me back to when we were young and Nana, Grandma or Mom would be frying eggplant, zucchini, cutlets or even meatballs, and we would sneak in the kitchen and grab some freshly fried from the paper towels and dip it in the sauce on the stove behind her back before it was served. It always seemed to taste better like that for some reason. These will quickly become a favorite for an easy crowd-pleasing snack, appetizer or side dish.

SERVINGS: 4-6 | Prep Time: 15 minutes | Cooking Time: 10 minutes

INGREDIENTS:

3 medium sized zucchini, at least 6-8 inches long
1 1/2 cups of all-purpose flour
4 large eggs
1 1/2 cups of panko bread crumps
1 1/4 cup freshly grated Parmigiano-Reggiano cheese
Vegetable, canola or grapeseed oil for frying
Salt and pepper, to taste

DIRECTIONS:

1. Wash and pat dry zucchini. With skin retained, slice zucchini into rounds of equal thickness. Using a slicer will give you the most consistent slices.

2. Remove as much liquid as possible from the sliced zucchini before frying. To do this, season with salt and let it sit for a few minutes. Then pat dry with a paper towel.

3. Pour enough oil into a large frying pan or skillet to reach a depth of 2 inches. Preheat over medium heat until a deep-fry thermometer reaches 350°F.

4. Combine 1 cup of the Parmigiano-Reggiano cheese, panko, salt and pepper into a medium bowl. Whisk the eggs in another bowl to blend. Add the flour into a third bowl. In batches, dip each slice of zucchini in the flour to coat completely. Then dip each into the egg, and allow the excess to drip off, and finally, dip the zucchini in the panko mixture, patting each to adhere and coat completely. Place each round into parchment paper on a cookie sheet.

5. Add the zucchini and fry for 4-5 minutes or until the zucchini is brown and crispy. Be sure to space out your zucchini in the pan and do not allow them to overlap. Arrange on a platter and sprinkle with the remaining cheese. Serve with marinara sauce. (See recipe for marinara sauce, page 29).

Brown Butter Bourbon Maple Candied Carrots

These buttery, boozy and sweet-as-candy carrots are the most addictive, glaziest carrots you'll ever eat. They are perfect to spruce up a holiday or any special occasion menu. After all, there aren't many things that smell better than the aroma of butter, brown sugar, and bourbon simmering on your stove. If you want to wow your guests and really play up your side-hustle this is the recipe you'll want.

SERVINGS: 6 | Prep Time: 10 minutes | Cooking Time: 15 minutes

INGREDIENTS:
2 pounds of baby carrots, peeled
3/4 cup of butter
1/2 teaspoon of salt or more, to taste
1/2 cup of bourbon whisky
1/3 cup of light brown sugar
2 tablespoons of maple syrup
1 tablespoon of chili-infused honey (or regular if you do not like spice)
1 cup of dried cranberries
1 teaspoon of cayenne pepper (if you like spice)
Freshly ground black pepper
2 sprigs of thyme to garnish

DIRECTIONS:
1. Melt the butter in a large deep skillet over medium-high heat. When the butter is foaming and brownish, add the carrots, followed by the salt and stir until the liquid from the carrots evaporates and they begin to brown around the edges, about 6-7 minutes.

2. Reduce the heat to medium-low and add the bourbon, while stirring. Cook for about 2-3 minutes until the alcohol has almost evaporated.

3. Add the brown sugar and stir until the carrots are almost cooked through, about 4 minutes. Add the cranberries, syrup and honey, stir to combine and let simmer for another 1-2 minutes, careful not to overcook the carrots.

4. When the carrots are nearly tender, raise the heat to medium-high so the glaze thickens, about 30 seconds.

5. Season with cayenne pepper and ground black pepper. Transfer to a serving bowl or dish and garnish with fresh thyme.

Nana's Sausage Stuffing

A longtime favorite for Thanksgiving, the jury is still out on whether this is actually a side dish or the main attraction. This stuffing is way too delicious to put in the bird. It's as rustic, rich and intense as I remember my Nana making it. A savory blend of Italian fennel sausage, the edges are golden and crunchy, and the inside is soft, flavorful and filled with herbs and pungent cheese.

SERVINGS: 8-12 | Prep Time: 20 minutes | Cooking Time: 1 hour and 20 minutes

INGREDIENTS:
14 cups of stale Italian bread small cubes - white, sourdough or white and wheat mix can work too
1 pound of sweet Italian sausage with fennel, out of casing
1 pound of hot Italian sausage with fennel, out of casing
2 cups of diced yellow onions
2 cups of diced celery
1 cup of diced carrots
2 tablespoons of extra virgin olive oil
1 cup of Pecorino Romano cheese
1 teaspoon of celery salt + extra, to taste
1 teaspoon of black pepper + extra, to taste
8 cups of low sodium chicken broth
10 tablespoons of butter (1 stick plus 2 tablespoons)
2 tablespoons of chopped parsley

*If you want to buy store bought you can use 2 12-ounce packages of Pepperidge Farm® Country Style Cubed White and Wheat. You can also use 14 cups of "fresh" dried stuffing cubes from Whole Foods® Market.

DIRECTIONS:
1. Preheat oven to 350°F. Place the bread cubes in a single layer on a sheet pan and bake for approximately 7 minutes. Set to the side.
2. In a large sauté pan, brown the sausage with 2 tablespoons of olive oil. While cooking, break apart the sausage into small pieces with a metal spatula or wooden spoon.
3. Melt a stick plus 2 tablespoons of butter in a large stock pot approximately 4 quarts or more over medium heat. Add the chopped onions, celery, and carrots.
4. Cook until vegetables are tender-crisp, about 8-10 minutes.
5. Add 6 cups of chicken broth to the cooked vegetables and bring to a boil. Add the celery salt and pepper. Remove from heat.
6. Stir in the baked bread cubes and fold in the browned sausage, Pecorino Romano cheese and parsley. Mix together thoroughly. At this point, I recommend sampling and adding salt or pepper to taste, if necessary.
7. Put oven on broil. Lightly butter the sides and bottom of a large 4-quart casserole dish or aluminum tin (whatever you're serving in). Transfer the mixed stuffing from the pot to the dish or tin and broil uncovered for approximately 10-15 minutes so the top is crispy and golden brown.

Notes:
• On the reheat, you may need to add more chicken broth as the stuffing tends to soak up the moisture.
• To reduce sodium in the recipe, you may substitute unsalted butter and use low salt chicken stock.
• If you cannot find sausage with fennel, I recommend using 2 teaspoons of fennel seeds and browning the sausage with them.
• If you do not prefer spice, you may use 2 pounds of sweet sausages instead.
• Bread can be toasted 3 days ahead and kept (once cooled) in a sealed bag at room temperature.
• Stuffing tastes best on the day you want to serve, but you can make stuffing ahead up to 1 day. Cover unbaked stuffing mixture in a large 4-quart casserole dish and refrigerate up to one day. Bake 30 minutes until hot.
• Stuffing also freezes well. Make sure it's cooled completely before freezing in an airtight container for up to 1-3 months. Best is to freeze it uncooked. When thawing, thaw in refrigerator overnight. Preheat your oven to 350°F.
• Place the stuffing into an oven-safe dish and cover with foil. To eliminate concern stuffing will be dry, drizzle some chicken broth and dot with extra butter prior to baking for 15 minutes.
• If your stuffing is too wet and gummy (this recipe shouldn't be) turn it out onto a baking pan or cookie sheet. Break it up and spread it into an even layer. Then bake until dried to the level you desire. Return the stuffing back into its dish and serve.
• You will probably need closer 8 cups of low sodium of chicken broth for the recipe. Low-sodium is very important since the added cheese provides a great deal of sodium.

Cranberry Sauce

This simple, fresh but mouth-watering recipe will make you wonder why you ever used store-bought cranberry in the past. Flavored with orange zest and chopped walnuts, it is the perfect side for roast turkey, chicken, ham and all the other classic holiday dishes. If you have any leftovers, topping toast or muffins with cranberry and mascarpone makes a simple and delicious post-holiday breakfast.

SERVINGS: 8-10 | Prep Time: 5 minutes | Cooking Time: 10 minutes

INGREDIENTS:
1 bag of cranberries, rinsed and drained (12 ounces)
1 cup of sugar
1 cup of water
1 teaspoon of tangerine or orange balsamic
1 teaspoon of orange zest
1/2 cup of chopped walnuts
1/4 teaspoon of ground cinnamon
Orange peel for garnish

DIRECTIONS:
1. Bring sugar and water in a medium saucepan to boil. Add the washed cranberries, orange zest, balsamic on low-medium heat. Return to a boil, stirring occasionally.

2. Reduce heat and boil gently for about 10 minutes, or until cranberries begin to burst and the sauce thickens. Cool completely at room temperature then refrigerate until serving. Add walnuts before serving.

Mashed Purple Sweet Potatoes

Sometimes a side dish is just a boring side dish but when your side hustle becomes the main attraction that's when the magic happens. You will keep coming back to this recipe as a savory bed for meats and chicken, or as a stand-alone dish which is so colorful and delicious that you can seriously eat it for breakfast.

SERVINGS: 2-4 | Prep Time: 5 minutes | Cooking Time: 15 minutes

INGREDIENTS:
3 large purple potatoes
1 tablespoon of extra virgin olive oil or vegetable spread
7 ounces or half of a can of coconut milk
2 tablespoons of maple balsamic vinegar (or 2 tablespoons of maple syrup)
1 teaspoon of brown sugar
1 teaspoon of ground cinnamon
Chopped walnuts or pecans for serving, if desired

DIRECTIONS:
1. Wash the potatoes, retaining skin, and prick them all over with a fork. Bring them to a boil in a medium pot of salted water.

2. Boil them until they are soft and you can pierce them with a fork. Remove them from the water and pat dry.

3. In a medium bowl, add the boiled potatoes and all other ingredients. Use a potato masher to mash until soft.

* This is actually a vegan and dairy-free recipe but you can definitely substitute butter for oil and regular milk for coconut milk in the same amounts.

I love helping people "disarm the kitchen." People who have always lacked confidence in the kitchen then beaming proudly because they have made one of my recipes makes me feel very accomplished.

I feel blessed to have the means to have healthy food to begin with, which many people do not have. Being creative and ingenious with different recipes while feeding others is most fulfilling to me.

Fiori di Sicilia Pistachio Olive Oil Cake

Like many Mediterraneans, I love a good citrus-flavored olive oil cake. This is a dessert that can be enjoyed at breakfast, for an aperitivo, or after dinner. It's a cross between a Greek Vasilopita New Year's Day cake (minus the hidden coin) and a traditional orange olive oil cake but contains chopped pistachios, pistachio extract and some sanguinello. The olive oil contributes a pleasant flavor while keeping the cake moist for longer than butter ever could. An elegant and fragrant treat all by itself, the hints of fresh orange zest coupled with the nutty pistachios will make this cake a new favorite in your house.

With one bite of the orange and pistachio combination, you'll feel like Remy in Disney's Ratatouille when he first takes a bite of a piece of cheese, which immediately creates an upbeat swirl of flavors and then separately takes a bite of the strawberry, sensing a lighter flavor. And then when he combines the two, they create a brilliant epiphany that sparking fireworks that dance and sparkle in his mind.

SERVINGS: 12 | Prep Time: 15 minutes | Cooking Time: 45 minutes

INGREDIENTS:

1 cup plus 2 tablespoons of all-purpose flour
2 teaspoons of baking powder
1/4 teaspoon of baking soda
1 cup of granulated white sugar
Zest of one orange
4 egg yolks and whites separated
1/3 cup plus one tablespoon of olive oil (butter-flavored olive oil if available)

1 1/2 teaspoons of Fiori di Sicilia extract
1/2 teaspoon of vanilla extract
1/2 cup of Greek yogurt
1/3 cup of ground pistachios plus additional for garnish
1 tablespoon of sanguinello (orange liquor)
Confectioners' sugar for serving

DIRECTIONS:

1. Preheat oven to 350°F.

2. In a medium bowl, mix the flour baking powder and baking soda.

3. In another bowl, mix the olive oil, orange zest, and sugar. Once combined, add the yogurt and mix well. Then add the fiori di Sicilia and vanilla extract and mix.

4. In a small bowl, mix the egg yolks with the sanguinello and add to the olive oil mix. Once blended, add the ground pistachios and mix well.

5. Add the flour mixture to the olive oil mixture, stirring until the flour has blended in but do not overmix, meaning mix with a spoon not an electric mixer.

6. Beat the egg whites until soft peaks form and then fold it into the batter.

7. Line the base of an 8" or 10" springform pan with wax paper. Grease the whole pan and sprinkle with flour or use oven bake spray.

8. Pour the batter in the pan.

9. Bake in the oven for about 40 to 50 minutes. The top of the cake will appear brown. Check with a toothpick to see if it is ready.

10. Remove from oven and let it cool. Remove from pan and let it continue to cool. Once completely cool, sprinkle with powdered sugar and additional ground pistachios if desired.

Chocolate Pots de Crème

When it comes to desserts, who doesn't love simple? These traditional classic French desserts are made of the most basic ingredients, most of which you likely have on hand already, and are so very easy to prepare. Often overshadowed by the popular Crème Brûlée, this French custard dessert, literally meaning "pots of cream," should receive way more recognition than they do. Even though these are served in adorable individual ramekin portions, one spoonful of the rich dark chocolate with a hint of chili, topped with whipped or iced cream, and I can guarantee you won't be able to stop at one!

SERVINGS: 4-6 | Prep Time: 30 minutes | Cooking Time: 40 minutes

INGREDIENTS:
1 1/2 cups of heavy cream
1 cup of whole milk
5 ounces of bittersweet chocolate, chopped
1/2 teaspoons of vanilla extract
3/4 teaspoons of cayenne pepper
1 pinch of salt
6 large egg yolks
1/3 cup of sugar
Ice cream or whipped cream to serve

DIRECTIONS:
1. Preheat oven to 325°F.

2. In a heavy, medium-size saucepan on medium, heat the cream and milk to just to a simmer. Remove from heat and add the chocolate. Whisk until melted and smooth, then add the vanilla, cayenne and salt.

3. In another bowl, whisk together the egg yolks and sugar. Whisk in the hot chocolate mixture a bit at a time. Let cool 10 minutes, then skim any foam from the surface.

4. Divide this custard among the baking dishes. Place them in a roasting pan with at least 2-inch sides. Pour warm water into the pan, enough to come halfway up the sides of the bakers.

5. Bake until the custards are set but the centers still move slightly when gently shaken, about 40 minutes. Remove from the water bath and chill until cold, a few hours. Cover and keep chilled until ready to serve. Add a dollop of whipped cream and chocolate shavings and voila!

Pistachio Cake

Growing up, this was THE cake my mom made for our birthdays each year, Now, the cycle repeats. A complete pistachio lover, one bite of this, and I'm instantly transported to my childhood. It's also a big family hit on St. Paddy's Day or Easter!

SERVINGS: Makes one 10" bundt cake | Prep Time: 10 minutes | Cooking Time: 50-60 minutes

INGREDIENTS:
1 box of yellow cake mix
2 (3.4 ounce) packages of instant pistachio pudding mix
1 cup of vegetable oil
3 eggs
1 cup of unflavored sodium free seltzer
1/2 cup of chopped pistachio nuts
1 (1.5 ounce) envelope of whipped topping mix (Dream Whip®)
1 1/2 cup of milk
6 drops of green food coloring (optional)

DIRECTIONS:
1. Preheat the oven to 350°F. Grease and flour a 10" bundt pan.

2. In a medium bowl, stir together the cake mix and 1 package of instant pudding. Add the oil, eggs and club soda and mix well. Fold in the chopped nuts, reserving some for garnish. Stir in the 6 drops of green food coloring, if desired, until fully incorporated. Pour into the prepared pan.

3. Bake for 50-60 minutes in a preheated oven, until cake springs back when lightly touched, and a toothpick comes out clean. Cool for 10 minutes in the pan before inverting onto a wire rack to cool completely. For the frosting, in a medium bowl, stir together the instant whipped topping and the other box of instant pudding. Add the milk and mix well until light and fluffy. Slice cooled cake into layers, fill and frost, including the hole in the middle. Garnish with pistachios. Keep chilled until serving.

Apple Dough-less Doughnuts

They look like donuts, they taste like donuts, but at their core, they're really apples! The next time you go apple picking with the kids and don't know what to do with all the bushels of apples you picked, aside from apple pie and baked apples, this is a super easy, healthy and delicious recipe to make, and afterwards, you can ask your guests how do they like those apples.

SERVINGS: Makes 12 doughnuts | Prep Time: 5 minutes | Cooking Time: 10 minutes

INGREDIENTS:
1 1/2 cups of flour
1 cup of rolled oats
1/4 cup of light brown sugar and 1/4 cup of dark brown sugar
1 teaspoon of baking powder
1 teaspoon of cinnamon plus additional for garnish
1/2 teaspoon of nutmeg
1 teaspoon of salt
1 egg
3 tablespoons of buttermilk
1/3 cup of milk
4 apples
2 cups of vegetable or grape seed oil, for frying
1/2 cup of confectioners' sugar, for coating

DIRECTIONS:
1. For the batter, mix together the flour, rolled oats, brown sugar, baking powder, cinnamon, nutmeg, and salt. Mix in the egg and buttermilk. Gradually stir in the milk. For the vegan prep with no dairy – you would just mix all the dry ingredients together – flour, oats, baking powder, brown sugar, cinnamon, nutmeg and salt.

2. Core the apples and slice vertically into thirds, for doughnut-size rings. Each apple should give you 3 rings.

3. Heat the oil in a deep frying pan to 350°F.

4. Evenly coat each apple slice, front, back and center hole, in the batter mix as if you were breading a chicken cutlet. If you are not using the batter and opting for the vegan preparation, pat each apple ring dry with paper towel and generously coat each ring with maple syrup or agave on both sides and in the hole, then dip into the dry mixture in Step # 1.

5. Carefully lay the doughnuts into the oil and fry for about 2-3 minutes on each side, until golden brown. Tong out and onto paper towel before coating in powdered sugar and cinnamon.

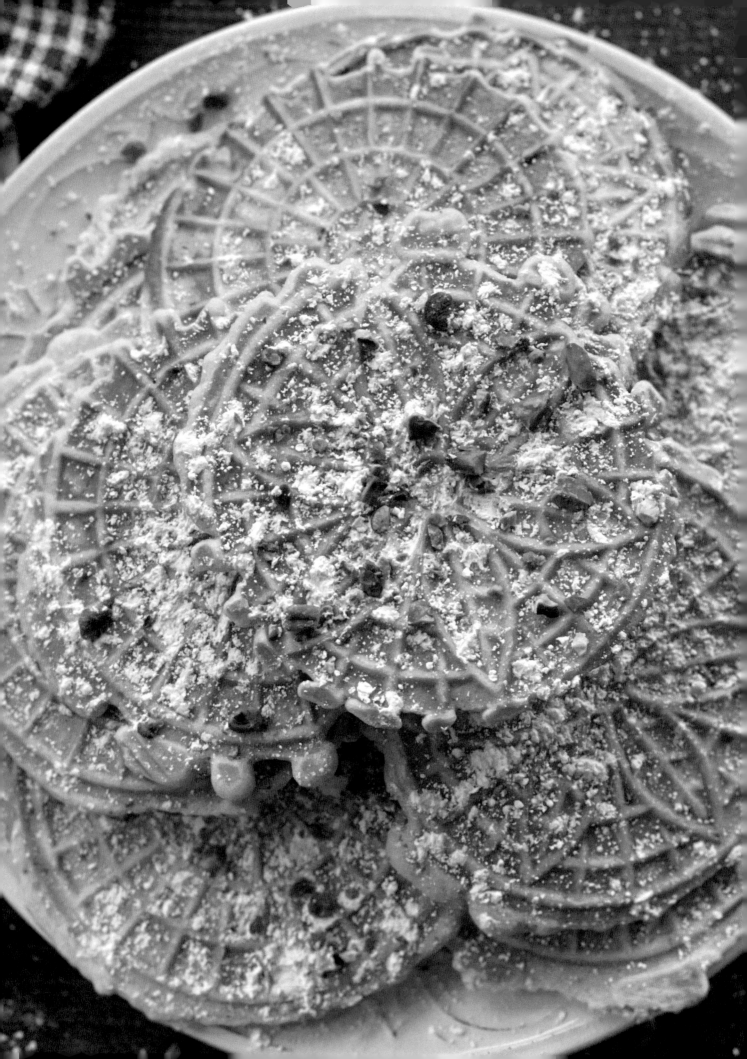

Pistachio Pizzelle

Pizzelle are the quintessential authentic Italian cookies made every year at Christmas or Easter-time in an assortment of flavors such as anise, lemon, almond and chocolate. I could not resist making these in pistachio, my weakness, and they have replaced anise as my all-time favorite flavor. Not only are they super flavorful, but they are a pretty shade of light green. So light and crispy, these make a perfect holiday gift in a classy dish or just a delicious addition to your dessert table. It is also common to sandwich two pizzelle with cannoli cream or hazelnut spread. While still warm, they can also be rolled using a wooden dowel to create cannoli shells.

SERVINGS: Makes about 30 pizzelles | Prep Time: 5 minutes | Cooking Time: 40 minutes

INGREDIENTS:

2 cups of all-purpose flour
4 large eggs
1 cup of granulated sugar
3/4 cup of butter, melted and cooled
1 teaspoon of pistachio extract
1 teaspoon of almond extract
2 teaspoons of baking powder
1 cup of chopped pistachio nuts
Confectioners' sugar, for serving
Green food coloring

DIRECTIONS:

1. Preheat pizzelle iron and lightly brush with nonstick cooking spray or vegetable oil. In a mixing bowl, combine flour, sugar, butter, extracts, baking powder, eggs, pistachios and a few droplets of green food coloring. Drop slightly rounded tablespoons of batter on to pizzelle iron and close.

2. Bake as directed by machine instructions or until golden brown, 30 seconds to 1 minute. Using a nonstick spatula, remove each pizzelle to a cooling rack; repeat with remaining batter.

3. Cool and sprinkle with confectioners' sugar and chopped pistachios, if desired.

Flourless Chestnut Chocolate Cake

Everyone needs a flourless cake in their lives and this is the one. This decadent cake has a marvelous texture that most flourless chocolate cakes have, but the addition of chestnuts provides an earthy and sweet, buttery, meaty texture which pairs seamlessly with dark chocolate. With a hint of rum and vanilla, and a dollop of the sweet chestnut cream purée on the side, you will wonder where this recipe has been hiding all your life.

SERVINGS: 8-12 | Prep Time: 10 minutes | Cooking Time: 40-50 minutes for cake and another 40-50 minutes for purée if roasting chestnuts.

INGREDIENTS:

6 eggs, separated
1/3 cup of granulated sugar
2 tablespoons of dark rum
1 pinch of salt
2 tablespoons of cocoa powder
1/2 cup of confectioners' sugar for dusting and to make extra cream for garnish
2 cups of unsweetened chestnut purée (see below) + 1/2 cup extra for garnish

1/2 cup of heavy cream
1 stick of unsalted butter, softened
1 teaspoon of vanilla extract
8 ounces of dark chocolate (60% or more of cacao)
1 teaspoon of vegetable oil

DIRECTIONS:

1. Preheat oven to 350°F and grease a spring form pan.
2. Chop the chocolate into pieces and melt it in the microwave or stovetop along with the cocoa powder and vegetable oil, careful not to burn. Set aside.
3. In a medium mixing bowl, whisk the egg whites with a pinch of salt until they are firm, but not dry.
4. In another medium mixing bowl, whisk the butter and chestnut purée with sugar.
5. Gradually whisk in the egg yolks, then add the chocolate, rum and vanilla extract.
6. Gradually stir in the egg whites, whisking well gradually to incorporate it into the chestnut mixture.
7. Pour the batter into the tin and let it bake for 40-50 minutes. Stick a toothpick in the center at around 40 minutes. If it comes out completely clean, then you can remove it from the oven.
8. Let the cake cool in the tin on a rack before you unmold it onto a platter.
9. Dust with confectioners' sugar and serve.

Chestnut Purée:

You can either purchase jarred, previously roasted deshelled (unsalted) chestnuts or roast your own. If the former, you will blend 2 1/2 cups of jarred chestnuts in a food processor or blender with a little bit of water to form a purée. If you are opting for the latter, you will need:

2 pounds of chestnuts + extra for the garnish
3 cups of water

DIRECTIONS:

1. Preheat oven to 450°F.
2. Cut a cross in the chestnuts with a knife and place on a cookie sheet and roast for 20-30 minutes.
3. Remove them with a towel and quickly peel the warm chestnuts.
4. Place the peeled chestnuts in a pan and add water.
5. Cook the chestnuts on high heat, while stirring, until all the water has evaporated and they are soft, approximately 10-15 minutes.
6. Empty the chestnut filling into a food processor or blender and add water until smooth.
7. Save about 1/2 cup of the puree for the garnish.

For the garnish: Combine 1/2 cup chestnut purée, the heavy cream and 1/2 cup confectioners' sugar. If the mixture seems too thin, add more sugar. If the mixture sees too thick, add more heavy cream. Refrigerate for 10 minutes to harden a bit.

Saturn Peach Dough-less Doughnuts

Last summer during the peak of Covid, I think my son and I must have hit every Farmer's Market in New Jersey since it was the one activity we could do without worry. We actually went peach picking a few times. Nothing tastes more like summer than ripe peaches. In our travels we saw Saturn Peaches. Aside from making jams and hot sauce, I thought these would be perfect for trying out the Apple Donut recipe on, and a star was born.

SERVINGS: Makes 4 peaches | Prep Time: 5 minutes | Cooking Time: 10 minutes

INGREDIENTS:
4 Saturn peaches
1 1/2 cups of flour
1 cup of rolled oats
1/4 cup of light brown sugar
1/4 cup of dark brown sugar
1/4 cup of white sugar
1 teaspoon of baking powder
1 teaspoon of cinnamon plus additional for garnish
1/2 teaspoon of nutmeg
1 teaspoon of salt
1 egg
3 tablespoons of buttermilk
1/3 cup of milk
2 cups of vegetable or grape seed oil, for frying
1/2 cup of confectioners' sugar, for coating

DIRECTIONS:
1. Press the pit out of each peach from the bottom to top so that each peach resembles a donut with a hole in the middle. Bring a medium pot of water to boil and blanch the peaches for about a minute. Then put the peaches in a bowl of ice water. Peel the skin off of each peach, which should remove pretty easily.

2. For the batter, mix together the flour, rolled oats, brown sugar, baking powder, cinnamon, nutmeg, and salt. Mix in the egg and buttermilk. Gradually stir in the milk. For the vegan prep with no dairy – you would just mix all the dry ingredients together – flour, oats, baking powder, brown sugar, cinnamon, nutmeg and salt.

3. Core the apples and slice vertically into thirds, for doughnut-size rings. Each apple should give you 3 rings.

4. Heat the oil in a deep frying pan to 350°F.

5. Evenly coat each apple slice, front, back and center hole, in the batter mix as if you were breading a chicken cutlet. If you are not using the batter and opting for the vegan preparation, pat each apple ring dry with paper towel and generously coat each ring with maple syrup or agave on both sides and in the hole, then dip into the dry mixture in Step # 2.

6. Carefully lay the doughnuts into the oil and fry for about 2-3 minutes on each side, until golden brown. Tong out and onto paper towel before coating in powdered sugar and cinnamon.

Pistachio Crème Brûlée

It probably doesn't get more classic than Crème Brûlée. While there's absolutely nothing wrong with this creamy French dessert made the traditional way, all its decadent vanilla bean custard splendor, I thought it was time to get a tad more creative and incorporate pistachios. Pistachios make everything better, right? Especially when they are pistachios from the pistachio mecca - Bronte, Sicily. The contrast between the cold custard and the hard, sugary layer of caramel goodness is what makes this dessert so irresistible. One bite of the pistachio undertones will have you hooked for life. The ideal dessert to make in advance if you're entertaining, but get ready to share the recipe, because you will be asked!

SERVINGS: 4-6 | Prep Time: 5 minutes | Cooking Time: 25 minutes (plus 4 hours to cool)

INGREDIENTS:
1 cup of chopped pistachios, plus 2 tablespoons extra for serving
2 cups of heavy cream
1 vanilla bean or 1 tablespoon of vanilla bean paste
1/2 teaspoon of pistachio extract
1/4 cup of honey
1/4 teaspoon of salt
4 egg yolks
1/4 cup of granulated sugar, plus additional for torching

DIRECTIONS:
1. In a food processor or with a hammer and zipper bag, grind the pistachios until finely chopped, careful not to create a paste.

2. In a small saucepan, combine the heavy cream, vanilla bean, pistachio extract, honey, salt and chopped pistachios. Bring the mixture to a simmer, stirring and then let it steep for about 25-30 minutes until all the flavors combine thoroughly.

3. In a medium bowl, gently whisk the egg yolks.

4. Preheat oven to 350°F, then place 4-6 ramekins or oven-safe dishes in a roasting pan filled with enough water to reach halfway up the sides of the ramekins.

5. Slowly add the warm cream mixture to the eggs while whisking.

6. Divide the custard equally among all the ramekins or dishes.

7. Carefully transfer the roasting dish to the oven and bake until the custard is just set around the edges but still a bit jiggly in the center, about 20-25 minutes.

8. Allow the custards to cool in the pan then refrigerate about 4 hours until set.

9. Sprinkle a thin, even layer of granulated sugar on all the custards. Use a cooking torch to melt the sugar on each of them. Add another thin layer of sugar and again use the torch to melt it on each of them, careful not to burn it. Add a third and final even layer of sugar, this time adding more, to each of the ramekins. Then torch it until it is a deep caramel color. Add the chopped pistachios to garnish and then serve right away. The custards can be made a few days in advance and refrigerated, but the torching should be done immediately prior to serving.

People who appreciate good food, drink, and a laugh are the best kind of people.

Passion. That's my secret ingredient.

Drinks

Raspberry Persimmon Smash

If you need a festive cocktail to get you in the holiday spirit, look no further. Not only is this drink colorful and will make your glass look pretty, it is a very balanced combination of tart and sweet with a delicate hint of mint and rosemary. If you really want to impress your guests with a signature holiday libation, this one will deliver. Delicious, nutritious and refreshing.

SERVINGS: 2 | Prep Time: 5 minutes

INGREDIENTS:
6 ounces of rye
2 sprigs of mint
2 teaspoons of agave (optional)
1 persimmon, skin removed
10 raspberries
Ice cubes
2 sprigs of rosemary for garnish
Starlino™ cherries

DIRECTIONS:
1. In each glass, muddle 5 raspberries, half of the persimmon, 7 mint leaves. When fully muddled, add 2 Starlino™ cherries in each glass plus 1 teaspoon of agave (if desired).

2. Add ice and rye and stir. Garnish with rosemary and a cherry.

Coquitos

It's not a party until the coquito arrives! Part beverage, part dessert, this traditional thick and creamy Christmas Puerto Rican coconut eggnog has been reinvented more than Madonna in recent years. No longer just an eggnog, coquito lends itself to being made in countless delicious flavors, such as pistachio and pumpkin. Perfect for any holiday or gathering, you will leave your guests dancing and wanting more. The great thing is that it's so easy to prepare, and you can store this recipe up to a month in the refrigerator, but good luck making it last that long!

SERVINGS: 8 cups | Prep Time: 5 minutes

INGREDIENTS:
1 can of sweetened condensed milk (14 ounces)
1 cup of white rum to start
2 egg yolks
1 can cream of coconut (15 ounces)
1 can of evaporated milk (12 ounces)
1 cup of unsweetened coconut milk (or from a fresh coconut)
1 teaspoon of vanilla extract
1/2 teaspoon of ground cinnamon
1/4 teaspoon of ground nutmeg and extra to sprinkle for serving
Cinnamon sticks for serving
Pinch of salt

DIRECTIONS:
1. Combine cream of coconut, condensed milk, evaporated milk, coconut milk, rum, eggs, vanilla, cinnamon and nutmeg in a blender and blend until smooth, about 2 minutes.

2. To transfer to a pitcher, cover tightly with plastic wrap and refrigerate for an hour. Coquito is best when it's very cold.

3. For the pumpkin pie version, add 1/2 cup pumpkin purée and 1/2 teaspoon of pumpkin pie extract plus extra cinnamon to the blender, and for the pistachio version, add 1/4 cups of chopped pistachios, 1/2 teaspoon of pistachio or almond extract, plus a drop of green food coloring to the blender.

"The Danielle"

If you are looking for Summer in a glass, you have found it. With refreshing sweet watermelon and leaves of fragrant garden basil, this cocktail smells as delicious as it looks and tastes. My cocktails always seem to have an element of produce incorporated in them, and this one is no exception. Working equally well with tequila or vodka, you can easily infuse this in a large dispenser or jug for larger parties.

SERVINGS: 2 | Prep Time: 5 minutes

INGREDIENTS:
3 slices of fresh watermelon, seeds removed, one is for garnish
12 leaves of fresh basil, some for garnish
Ice cubes
2 teaspoons of agave
6 ounces of blanco tequila

DIRECTIONS:
1. Take 2 of the 3 slices of watermelon and cut into cubes and muddle the equivalent of one slice in each glass, plus one teaspoon of agave and 5 leaves of basil in each glass and muddle together thoroughly.

2. Add ice then add tequila and stir. Garnish with a small watermelon wedge and basil leaves.

Blood Orange Spiced Mulled Cider with Bourbon

Hot mulled cider is a must-have at all fall and winter gatherings. Living in New York, the frigid winters necessitate lots of cozy hot beverages, curled up with a good book or in front of a blazing fire. With fragrant notes of anise, cloves, cinnamon and cardamom, this mulled cider is just so delicious and inviting that you will be tempted to make it even in milder temperatures. Guests never seem to refuse a mug, especially the adults, who do a little self-spiking with their alcohol of choice. I prefer it with bourbon, but for parties, it's nice to keep that on the side so the kids can enjoy some as well.

SERVINGS: 8 | Prep Time: 5 minutes | Cooking Time: 20 minutes

INGREDIENTS:
2 quarts of apple cider
8 cinnamon sticks
2 whole allspice berries
2 whole cloves
6 star anise
1/4 teaspoon of nutmeg
7 pods of cardamom
1 whole blood orange, thinly sliced with the peel
1/4 cup of fresh cranberries
12-16 ounces of bourbon (1 shot per serving)

DIRECTIONS:
1. Simmer apple cider into a large saucepan, cover, turn the heat on medium-high. While the cider is heating up, add the rest of the ingredients except for the cinnamon sticks into a sachet or mesh tea infuser ball and drop into the cider. Keep covered and heat the mulled cider mixture to a simmer and reduce the heat to low. Simmer for 20 minutes on low heat.

2. Serve hot, ladling into mugs. Add a cinnamon stick to each cup.

Spicy Black Cat Cocktail

This is a black cat you will definitely want to cross your path. A spiced, cherry-flavored brandy-based cocktail popular around Halloween, but it is easy enough to prepare and enjoy for a happy hour or a gathering all year long. The Starlino™ or Luxardo®
cherries are a must-have on your bar for this and many other drinks!

SERVINGS: 2 | Prep Time: 5 minutes

INGREDIENTS:
2 ounces of spiced rum
2 ounces of vodka
4 ounces of cranberry juice
4 ounces of Dr. Pepper®
Luxardo® or Starlino™ cherries

DIRECTIONS:
1. Fill 2 glasses with ice.

2. In a shaker, add spiced brandy, cranberry juice, vodka and soda.

3. Shake vigorously. Pour into rocks glasses and garnish with cherries.

Food makes people happy, it takes you back home, it says so many things that words can't say. - Sophia Loren

My Nieces

Luca

Me & Mom

The

Cousin Sue & I

My Happy Place

Sis & Bro-In-Law

Pop Pop & Luca

Family

Me & Sean

My fur baby Aspen

Me & My Boy

A Note of Thanks

Although too many cooks in the kitchen may spoil a meal, I can honestly say that authoring a cookbook takes a village! It is a ton of work and I am very fortunate to have such a great team in my corner to help me along this first cookbook journey.

To Mom, Dad and Sis - I am blessed to still have you all around, and from the bottom of my heart, I thank you and Nana Angie and Grandpa Tommy, and Grandma Susie and Grandpa Vinny, who have left us. You have nurtured my love of food since the day I was born. Not only have you always supported my life journey and encouraged me to be my overachiever-Type-A self, but every day you taught me and continue to teach me that, with faith, grit and determination, nothing is impossible.

To Luca - my son, my love, my life and my every day food taster. I hope that you are half as proud of me as I am of you. I dedicate this compilation to you so that you may know and appreciate our family roots and Italian-American culture. May you always foster your budding passion for food that you've had from a very young age. I would love to see you cook for your own family someday, so that with each passing generation, our foodie legacy is preserved (and please make sure your future relationship passes the help-your-mom-with-the-dishes test!)

To Sean - thank you for always believing in me and being seatbelted next to me on this roller coaster of a ride when I decided to write a cookbook in the middle of a pandemic. Thank you for your invaluable tasting and advice, helping me decide from my 8000 photos for each recipe, for your tastebuds and "eye", terrace, cabinets, use of your kitchen, and allowing me in your space, both physically and emotionally, as a lawyer-turned-culinary artist, but mostly as your friend and trusted partner.

To "Cousin" Joe (Wizard Design Studios) and Cousin Sue - I love the fact that, in the true Italian way, we kept it in the family. Just this once, we'll allow readers to ask us about our family business! You both have been invaluable in the ideas, creation, design, and layout, of this cookbook from its inception. Despite your busy lives, you kept this project über organized and on track. It was such an added bonus that you're both tremendous foodies yourselves so it never really felt like work. And I apologize for getting you hungry at all hours of the day! The gratitude I feel to have you both is tremendous - you rock!

To Ornella Fado - thank you so much for supporting and believing in me from the day I informed you that I was pivoting into the culinary world from the legal one. As a successful and down-to-earth Italian working mom living in America, you are the epitome of beauty and brains, an inspiration to all, and I wholeheartedly appreciate you writing my Forward and forever being included in this book through your kind words.

To Anna Cabrera, my copy editor and trusted colleague, for patiently guiding me as a first-time author through the book-writing process. I am grateful to you for recognizing how personal these stories and recipes are to me.

The pandemic caused me to experience one of the most unpredictable and harrowing circumstances of my life. It also required me to be away from my professional life as a lawyer. I have introspectively unwrapped my gift and passion for cooking during this pause - I was given lemons and made lemonade that I am now sharing with the rest of the world. Have U Covered in the Kitchen is here to stay!

About the Author

Danielle Caminiti is an experienced attorney of over two decades, entrepreneur, culinary artist, food writer, blogger, brand ambassador, and most importantly, mother of her son, Luca. She is a seasoned legal professional who graduated from Fordham University School of Law and New York University, both with honors. Ms. Caminiti is also a former prosecutor of the Kings County District Attorney's Office. Additionally, she is a former associate of a prestigious medical malpractice defense firm, as well as a boutique commercial litigation firm, both in Manhattan.

Since 2013, Ms. Caminiti has been self-employed as a per diem attorney who covers virtual and in-person appearances and depositions regularly in New York City and State for hundreds of well-known law firms and solo practitioners. In 2019, Ms. Caminiti formed Have U Covered, LLC, which, like her recipes, she built from scratch. She is the solo owner of her Queens-based office, and together with her team of reliable and competent attorneys, she covers court cases in all 62 counties in New York State.

Having grown up in a closely knit Italian-American family in New York City, Ms. Caminiti has always had a genuine appreciation for Italian food and culture. Aside from domestic travel, she has traveled to Italy several times, as well as Greece, Africa, Spain, Turkey and Mexico. Danielle has always been an avid home cook, and although her cooking reflects strong ties to her Italian roots, she often ventures outside her comfort zone and embraces fusion cooking and dishes from other cultures. It makes her happy to feed people and she is truly in her element when entertaining family and friends with her culinary delights, a glass of wine, good conversation, and a lot of laughter.

Have U Covered LLC was put on an extended pause when the courts closed in March 2020 due to Covid-19. It remains uncertain whether and to what extent her business will return since success of her business depended a great deal on high volume of in-person court appearances. Despite this, Ms. Caminiti tells her clients that until she can have them covered in the courtroom again, she'll have them covered in the kitchen, and even if court returns to what it was pre-pandemic, she will always have them covered in the kitchen.

Made in the USA
Monee, IL
04 January 2022

350a5108-d352-44ae-82f4-3b2666d9b57aR01